FROM
MUD PIES
and
LILAC LEAVES

Bud-

We wouldn't trade those days
for anything, would we?

Bill Shrout

Photo on book jacket
taken about 1937
with a camera that cost
thirty-nine cents

FROM
MUD PIES
and
LILAC LEAVES

Bill Shrout

ℏℨℙ

HONEYBIL PUBLISHING

Post Office Box 2806
Clackamas, OR, 97015

Dedicated To the three women of my life:

First

to Mother, the content of this book will show my admiration and appreciation for her advice on how to live life to the fullest.

Second

to Julie, my loving and persistent wife, without her periodic push and gentle shove I would not have finished this work.

And thirdly

to Linda, my daughter, who planted the idea of *From Mud Pies and Lilac Leaves* and convinced me that I could write it.

CONTENTS

CONTENTS

3

LITTLE BILLY GOES TO SCHOOL
PAGE 61

4

PETS and OTHER CRITTERS
PAGE 87

5

YOUNG IMPRESSIONS
PAGE 115

6

BILLY'S ENTERPRISES
PAGE 143

7

FUN THINGS
PAGE 157

CONTENTS

10
FUN AT FRANK'S

Something about Frank
"Keep the Hell out"
Working for Frank
Snake in the Bucket
Frank's School House Potatoes
Frank and the C.C.C. Boys

11
HIGH SCHOOL and WORLD WAR II

Rationing
Homer and the Scrap Drive
School Teachers Are Not All Bad
High School Days and World War II
Downtown with Current Affairs and "Square Root"

EPILOGUE

PROLOGUE

Mother must have been a genius. She did not have all the usual credits that geniuses are known to possess. Her only accomplishments that man can measure were never officially recorded. The little one room school that she attended for a short while in Kentucky did not attempt to keep lasting records of its students. Mom made it known to me at an early age that she only went through the fourth reader of McGuffey's. She did not let this cause any disparagement in her approach to life with all of its distractions and monuments of decisions that needed to be made. She always seemed to have an answer. I can hear her voice of conscience today almost as clearly as it was personally given to me as a little boy growing up in Indiana. She would say, "Billy, be sure to remember all of the things you see today. If it doesn't work for someone else don't do it. There will be some things that you will see and hear that may be just the thing you might need later in life. If some want to make a mess of things, don't think for a minute that you have to follow after them".

Sometimes today I find myself thinking, "What would Mom do?" Then I realize that she, in her own way, had imparted wisdom and understanding for me to draw upon as I faced various encounters and times of stress. I call myself a student of reminiscence. Looking backwards is not all bad. For it is within the rearward glance that we are able to focus on the fruits of the great teacher, "experience". From this type of commitment I find that I am able to draw upon it in much detail and develop this chronicle.

1

LITTLE BILLY

My Beginnings

I began life as the last child of seven living children of a sharecropper farmer in Northern Indiana in 1926. My mother's pregnancy prior to the one that produced me ended in a stillbirth. My early days growing up were in the famous thirties, the era of The Great Depression. A sharecropper is just as the name implies; you share the crops that you might grow with the real owner of the land. Many different arrangements were made between share-cropper and owner as to the percentages of sharing. Corn might be 60/40 or hay 50/50, etc. In our case, we received pasture privileges and got to keep all of the milk

3

check. Dad owned the cows. The same also went for the hogs we raised. Those were days before much was known about commercial fertilizer; much value was placed on animal waste and the use thereof. A landlord would rather you keep livestock and use the animal waste to enrich the soil.

This will set the scene for some tales and yarns that I remember as I grew up.

I was born in Northern Indiana about 60 miles south of the Michigan border, in the middle of the state in a very small farming community by the name of Akron. This area is called North-Central Indiana and is located in Fulton County. This part of Indiana is known for the numerous small farms that dot the landscape. There are sufficient gentle rolling hills and swampy muck lands to break up any possibility of the larger flat stretches of land becoming too monotonous to its inhabitants.

Numerous small game lakes hide themselves here and there and add to the delight of the fisherman. They also became to many of us a huge bathtub for cleansing our farm dirtied bodies as we worked the Indiana fields in the summertime.

My father lived on a series of farms as he share-cropped his way through Indiana. I was born on the farm we called The Old King Place. A man by the name of Jake King owned the one hundred-sixty acre farm. The farm was located approximately two miles south and west of Akron. I went out there recently and looked around. All of the buildings are gone, but it was very nostalgic to walk into the lush corn field and stand where my father on an earlier occasion had told me where the house had stood. I thought about a Monday morning in a long ago October. In the middle of corn cutting season, I made my entry into the world. My dad and my oldest brother, Forrest, were cutting corn. The rest of my brothers and sisters were in school. Mother was washing clothes in the old rock-a-bye washer when she felt the first pains of the birthing process. Forrest came to the house and finished the washing. Dad went to town for Doc Ferry and I was born late in the morning. I happen to have in my scrapbook the canceled check for my total cost, made out to Dr. John Ferry, for twenty five dollars!

Four months later the family moved to another sharecrop situation, a place we fondly called The Old Shewman Farm. This farm was located two and one quarter miles east of Akron, Indiana, still in Fulton County. The farm was owned by a man named W.D. Shewman who lived in Webster Groves, Missouri. The fact that the landlord lived far enough away from the community that he only made rare trips to visit was indeed an unusual way to conduct business.   Each spring Dad would have one of the children write a letter for him to Mr. Shewman.   In the letter he would describe what he thought should be planted in each field.   Mr. Shewman would always respond in positive agreement. Later, it became my task to do the letter writing. We always referred to our landlord as "Mr. Shewman." He was a school teacher. When he wrote to my dad, it was always "Mr. Shrout" this or that. To me, a school teacher was high on the list of respected professionals.   To witness him calling my dad "Mr." really made me proud of my father's occupation.   I will always remember the funeral of Mr. Shewman. It seemed more like a eulogy to my dad than to the one who had died. In gathering the facts for the sermon, the minister found many excellent comments on behalf of my dad.

The Shewman farm was comprised of 120 acres. Some of it was hilly, rocky and not too fertile. There was a part of the farm that was in muck, decayed vegetation that has at one time or other been under water. Sometimes the water was tiled or open-ditched away from the property. Other instances it appeared that the water dried up on its own. Most of the muck land that we had would have water very close to the surface, perhaps only a foot or so beneath the surface of the ground.

As a farm goes, one could not say that it was very productive. If my father would have had the opportunity to farm a piece of land that was very fertile, he would have undoubtly reached his goal of owning his own land much sooner. But Dad was frugal and worked at whatever he was doing with much enthusiasm. His days were long in the fields.

I recall as if it were yesterday the layout of the farm buildings on the Shewman farm. The barn stood on a slight hill. The floor level at the back of the barn was a few feet higher than the cow lot that was immediately behind. The concrete foundation at the rear of the barn formed a concrete bank. Farmers referred to this type of construction as being a bank barn. Whenever we would take wagon loads of hay into the barn, we would have to go up the slight grade and onto the wooden barn floor. It had a hay mow on either end and two driveways between. Horse stalls and calving pens were on one side and the cow milking parlor on the other. There was a lean-to garage and corn crib added to the cow milking area on the north side. The barn was roofed with real slate. On a couple of occasions a piece of roof slid off to the ground, and I used it as a slate like my dad said he used when he was a boy in school.

The Shewman farmhouse, cob shed, well house, milk house and the lilac bush next to the highway.

The Shewman farm barnyard showing the milk house, well house, barn, granary and hen house.

A large two story house with a cemented cellar was approximately 175 feet to the south of the barn. There was no running water in the house, and consequently, no bath facilities. We had no electricity, and, in fact, depended on kerosene, or, as we called it, "coal oil."

We used the coal oil to fuel regular wick lamps. Later, a new type of mantel lamp called an Aladdin lamp, was used. I remember how wonderful we thought this new kind of lighting for the home was. The brilliance from this Aladdin lamp was many times more brilliant than the wick lamp. One had to be very careful in handling the lamp because the mantel was very delicate. When a new wick was installed, a lighted match was used to burn off the protective coating. From then on, the least little extra shake or bobble might cause the mantel to collapse.

The main floor of the house was made up of four large rooms, each wall finished attractively for its day in wainscoting that exhibited elaborate workmanship. Many layers of paint had graced the paneling since its first construction until the Shrouts moved in. We added several layers in the seventeen years we lived there. The upstairs was made up of one small and three large bedrooms.

We had an outside privy (toilet) , we referred to as the "three-holer." There were two holes for adults and a smaller one closer to the floor for us kids. When the pit would fill up, Dad would dig another pit and simply move the toilet. This seemed to be adequate for all of the years that we lived there.

Little Billy sitting on a Model T Ford at the Shewman farm. The lilac bush of the story is directly behind him.

Me in a Play Pen

The earliest that I can remember about my child-hood, I'm on the floor. As a little guy, I was not able to push or climb over a couple of chairs placed on their sides in the doorway between the dining room and the kitchen. My mother used this as an early make-do playpen to keep me away from the kitchen range or other dangerous areas in the house. I must have been less than one year old. I can vividly see the kitchen and my mother working by kerosene light, making breakfast for my dad and my brothers while they were doing the morning milking. Most of my memories of this event indicate that it was very early in the morning and the kitchen was lighted by a small coal oil lamp sitting on the large kitchen table. Mother is standing over the kitchen range and I can almost feel the pleasant warmthness of the fire that Dad had started earlier before going to the barn. I experienced early in life the welcome aromas that Mom was able to create with her cooking.

Many times over the years, I have had some interesting conversations with my family regarding this time in my life. It seems to be very unusual and almost unbelievable that I can remember being so young. The early morning time in the kitchen with my mother stands out in my memory.

Curly the Dog

I recall a dog we had when I was still very small. His name was Curly. My mother would do the unthinkable thing of putting that small dog up to the table and pretending to feed him his breakfast. More than likely, she was just entertaining me. This type of activity would not have met with much favor with the rest of the family. I am sure my mother would not have actually fed Curly at the table, but, in her way, she thought this was cute. It did make a lasting impression on me.

Not long after this memory, Curly was run over on the road in front of the house. My mother, in later years, told me about this and also informed me that I couldn't have been more than one and a half or two years old at the time of the dog's death. I remember Mother and me taking some sulfur matches and using them to decorate a cross she had made from a couple of pieces of crude wood. We took the cross and placed it on Curly's grave. When a person shows compassion and sensitivity in the fashion that my mother did, memories stay forever.

My Red Wagon

The Christmas of thirty-two saw me receiving a beautiful red coaster wagon. To this day I do not know how my parents arranged to find the necessary funds to make such a purchase in this time of the Great Depression. I remember thinking that this must be the largest red wagon ever made. I was so proud of it. I could not wait to take it out in the yard, but the snow was still deep and I had to wait. I would push the wagon carefully around in the house wherever Mom would let me. When the snow cleared away on the ground, I eagerly hurried forth to use my new friend in assisting Dad in some of his chores. I used my new wagon for the first time to haul a bushel of corn from the corn crib to the hog lot. Dad went with me of course and did the heavy work. I believe he was as proud of the wagon as I was.

My brother, Adrian, in later years, reminded me of an incident involving my wagon. Adrian and another brother, Irvin, found some nests of young mice and destroyed about a hundred of them. They thought it to be great sport to load them up in my wagon. I did not take to well to this and reported the deed to my mom. She made my brothers empty and clean the wagon.

13

Another use that was made of the red wagon was in slopping the hogs. Adrian would put the five-gallon slop bucket that contained dish water and leftover table scraps in the rear of the wagon and I would sit in the front of it. The wagon handle would stick up between my legs and I would use it to steer as Adrian pushed the wagon

Adrian and Billy just before they slopped the hogs.

with a stick. I thought this to be great fun even though Adrian would go fast and some of the slop would splash on me. On the farm, nothing was wasted and table scraps were fed to the hogs. They sure liked it for they always fought over it as they pushed one another around at the hog trough.

I kept the red wagon for several years. I remember using the rear portion as a trailer for my bike. The running gears were used over and over in making interesting play vehicles. They seemed to never wear completely out. This was the only wagon I ever had and I did make good use of it.

Wash Your Feet, Billy

The muck fields seemed to contribute the most noticeable dirt to our bodies after working in them. Muck is black and, when mixed with body perspiration, clings. Our entire bodies got dirty, but my mom only seemed to be concerned about our legs and feet. I guess she could easily see that they became dirty.

Hay making was another dirty job. Working in the hay mow was the dirtiest assignment. We had no running water. Sometimes we would head to nearby Rock Lake for a dip to remove the dirt. We did not use soap; swimming and splashing in the water seemed to take care of things.

On the evenings that we did not go to the lake, Mom would command, "Wash your feet, Billy." This meant that I was to take a wash pan full of cold water out of the drinking water bucket or the stove water reservoir and take it outside. The cement step felt warm from the summer sun to my bare feet. On a certain spot on the cement step that faced the road I would sit down with my pan of water. I would set the pan of water between my legs and roll up the legs of my coveralls. I would place my warm dirty feet, one at a time, into the wash pan. After getting most of the dirt off I would empty the pan and go to bed. Recently I had the opportunity to visit the old farm place. I walked to the very spot where I had washed my feet so many times. I could almost see the water trickling down the cement gutter that was still there beside the house.

I think of all of the modern conveniences that I take for granted. But as a child, I wished for even a simple thing like one light bulb to hang down from the kitchen ceiling. I would have been very pleased if our landlord would have run electric to the well house. Then dad would not have had to work so hard to keep the old John Deere engine going. Dad would get so frustrated when it wouldn't run. The rest of us would note as we came by the well house that tools were flying here and there and would quickly inform the rest of the family to be careful if they had to go by the door. Dad usually was pretty cool. But the old gas engine that pumped the water for the livestock tested him on several occasions. One time Dad made the mistake of striking a match to see if the pump's refusal to run might be lack of gasoline. He came close to a bad accident. It burned his eyebrows, singed his hair and came very close to damaging his eyes. There must have been someone in Akron that could have worked on the engine but these were the times of no cash and if you had something that needed fixing, you did it yourself.

The Old Spring Wagon

Every time I see an old buckboard wagon in a western movie I am reminded of the one-horse spring wagon we had on the Shewman farm. For all practical purposes it was used to make short trips and to haul small loads.

Irvin, Little Billy, Christeen and our dog.

18

The seat was made to accommodate two people and had a spring under it to make it ride smoothly as the wagon bounced over ruts and chuck-holes as it moved along. Mother would wrap me in a blanket and the two of us would go to the field with Dad on certain occasions. I remember lying in the bottom of the wagon box while Mom would help Dad do whatever tasks they had come to the field to do. I could not have been very old. I am sure Mother did not stray too far from the wagon and would have come running at the least peep out of me.

Many times I saw Dad hitch Charley, the horse, to the spring wagon and go into Akron on a few errands. The wagon was small but could haul a few bags of feed or several boxes of groceries if needed. We had a neighbor who lived about two miles east of us who could be seen on a regular basis, perhaps every two weeks or so, driving his two horse team and large hay wagon to Akron. He would put a couple straight chairs in the wagon and he, along with his wife, would be sitting up as pretty as you please enjoying their outing into the city. I do not think he had an automobile.

2

NEIGHBORS

About the Neighbors

When I think back about the neighborhood that I lived in, I'm amazed at the wide variety of personalities that lived there. Today, I hardly know my neighbors even though they live much closer. I may know them by name and some of what they do for a living. Some may be retired or work at this or that. When I was growing up on the Shewman farm, we not only knew the neighbors by their first and last names, but we also knew how old they were. The period of time of my growing up, and of my going to grade school, seemed to last forever as I lived it then. Each day seemed as though it would take a month to finish. All of our neighbors, as well as ourselves, had lived in the neighborhood for a long time. Some of our neighbors never moved the entire time we lived at the Shewman farm. People did not move about much in those days. I now realize that the reason I can recall such vivid memories of my childhood is the fact that my neighborhood was my whole world. I had very few distractions from the world about me. I followed my mother's instruction to the letter, and that was to remember what I saw and to remember it well. All of these good farm folk of my childhood are precious in my memory. Any peculiarities noted or mentioned are those of a small farm lad, just watching and listening to what went on around and about him.

Watermelons and Those Who Steal

My dad was probably one of the finest farmers in Northern Indiana. Dad's genius in farming transferred to the watermelon patch. I think he had a way of choosing the right horse manure to put into the planting hills. He would use a hoe and hill up the dirt about six inches across and four inches high. At the base of this hill he would place just the right quantity of specially selected horse manure. He leveled the top of the hill with the hoe and then placed several watermelon seeds on the hill. I was always fascinated with the way he did this. This procedure seemed to produce the finest tasting watermelons in our part of Indiana. Dad's reputation grew to where he was famous for this delicious repast.

The boys at school liked to discuss their experiences of the previous evenings. Some of these stories were about the girls, while others early in the school season would brag about whose watermelon patch they were in. On one occasion my brother, Irvin, heard the fellows discussing a certain patch that sounded as though it might be in our neighborhood. The city boys thought that they were in Homer Saner's patch, but the more Irvin listened, the more sure he was that they were talking about Dad's patch. The Akron boys made plans to hit this wonderful melon patch again that very evening. Irvin came home after school and told Dad. Dad and my brothers were waiting for them, hiding in the patch along the fence row. We had a 20-gauge shotgun that we kept around the farm to hunt crows and a rabbit once in a while. The shotgun was the weapon that Dad would use to beef up his authority with the watermelon thieves. Dad had his trusty comforter on this particular evening and caught the Akron lads in the act of stealing his watermelons. He took the boys to the house

23

at gun point and threatened to call the sheriff. The boys begged and pleaded for him not to call the law or their parents. After letting them squirm for a bit, Dad let them go.

One particular night of watermelon stealing stands out strong in my memory. It seemed that several different groups of young men from several different neighborhoods decided to hit the Shrouts' melon patch on the same night. Dad and some of my older brothers solicited aid from our neighbor, Ted Dilsaver. Ted was a tall, lanky man who owned a scary looking long-barreled rifle. I was too small to participate. I would listen in and run from window to window watching the show that went on in view of the house. Mom and I became brave enough to go out into the back yard. It was after dark, but we could see and hear almost everything since the melon patch was not all that far away. When lights would flash or someone would run into a barbed-wire fence, we knew just what had happened. Dad loaded Ted Dilsaver and his big rifle into our 1926 Model T Ford and started down the road very slowly. Dad had heard how the thieves communicate with the driver of the pick-up car. He was to blink the headlights of the car and that was the signal some of the thieving groups had prearranged with the drivers of their cars. What a surprise to the boys as they came out of the patch with melons under each arm to be greeted by big Tall Ted and his gun. Some of the melons they had carried out and

24

piled alongside of the road. Dad did not need to waste them. The young men had done a pretty good job of picking the ripe ones. Dad took them to the house and put them in the front yard to sell.

Yoo Hoo Vinnee

We had neighbors that lived across the huckleberry swamp. It couldn't have been more than 400 yards from one house to the other. The neighbor's name was Royer. Mrs. Royer's first name was LaVinna but we all called her "Vinnee." We were at times the only house in the imme-diate area that had a telephone. I can still see and hear my mother going out into the yard beside our house, cupping her hands and shouting, "Vinnee, yoo hoo, Vinnee." In just a short while we would hear back, "Laura, yoo hoo, Laura." It seems to me my mother's name always came out sound-ing like "Lau-ree." They would shout messages back and forth, most often wanting to know if they were going to be home. Neither would want to walk the treacherous path through the swamp if the other one was not going to be home. The Royer house could be reached by driving or walking down a long lane or by walking the dangerous path. The swamp had black snakes and once in a while one would see a blue racer snake. Rattlesnakes were in the area but did not favor places with a lot of water. Mom and Vinnee never let the snakes deter them. When any of us wanted to go to the other's place, we usually followed the fence row that divided the north hog lot from the south lot. After repeated crossings, a path soon developed.

On many of Mother's crossings of the swamp, I would accompany her. I was still quite small so this was an outing for me, and Mom could keep an eye on my whereabouts.

Run, Billy, Run

The trips that I made with my mom to the Royer's were perhaps some of the more eventful happenings in my growing up. After all, we did not have a working radio much of the time. Television had not made its appearance. With no daily paper to read the funnies out of, I was stuck with going with Mom. Arriving at their house usually meant a greeting by Vinnee's dog, Tutie. I liked dogs and found this part of the visit to be rewarding. I would listen to my mom and her friend talk about what was happening in their lives and found even that conversation to be somewhat interesting.

On one occasion I remember hearing a loud thud coming from the front part of the Royer house. Jess was Vinnee's husband and, unknown to Mom and me, he had been ill. Jess tried to get up from his bed and walk out to the kitchen for help. He didn't make it. We ran into the living room and there was Jess on the floor gasping his last breath. My Mother shouted, "Run, Billy, run and get Dad." Vinnee did not have a telephone and there was no way of calling for any professional help. Dad would have to do, and I knew this even at my age. You should have seen me sail over the fences and the mud holes and skim past the thorny bushes. I made much haste to the part of the barn where Dad was doing the evening chores. I remember calling to Dad, "Come quick, Dad, Jess is on the floor and is kicking bad." Dad and I ran back to the Royer house. Jess died right there on the living room floor. All of this was reinforced in my memory with one of Indiana's famous summer electrical storms.

Later, as I lay awake in the dark upstairs of the Shewman farm house, with all the booming of the thunder and the sharp flashing of the lightning, I could still see old Jess on the floor kicking and gasping for his very last breath. Jess's funeral was the second one that I recall going to. I could take you this very day to the grave spot where they buried old Jess. The first funeral I attended was for a man who was killed by an automobile on the road between our house and Akron. To this day I marvel how some events stay in such detail and portray themselves in such living color.

Becky and the Bull

One of the closest neighbors we had was Becky. Becky lived just to the north of us, across the field that Dad always seemed to have planted in alfalfa. I do remember a time or two that he had corn in this field. Old State Highway #114 went very close to the edge of the field. When the new paved road was completed and the sharp curves taken out, Becky's property was left with a lot of small unused portions of old highway running through it. These old roads soon became merely paths and were excellent means of walking back and forth between our houses. I also found the old roads a very good place to play and ride my bike.

Becky was a widow lady who remained by herself on the farm. Her children had long since left and were married and had their own places. Becky always wore a large straw hat with a big wide brim. When Mom and I would go to visit her, she would come out of her screened-in porch with that hat on and an apron around her waist. Outside her screened-in porch, she had a windmill that fascinated me. Pumping water on the Shewman farm was always such a chore. Either the pump would not work or we would have to pump hundreds of gallons of water by hand. I would watch the large wheel high in the air, spinning around ever so slowly, and there it was, a nice small stream of the coldest water trickling down .

Becky, with the help of one of her sons who lived nearby, managed to keep the farm going. She milked a small herd of milk cows. Most farmers who had a herd of ten or more cows would keep a bull to breed their cows. Becky never felt that her herd was large enough. About once a year, a cow would decide that she had been milked long enough and she would rather have a new offspring started. In those days, we referred to it as the cow going dry and coming into heat.

Dad had an arrangement with Jack Morris, the local livestock dealer, to board one of Jack's young bulls. Each year Dad would get a new bull from Jack. This kept new

stock and a new blood line in our herd. Becky's arrangement with my dad to use our bull was of long standing.
The plan was there and ready to go when one of Becky's
cows made the "I want a calf" move. When this happened,
Mom always seemed to be looking out of the north window
in the kitchen and would see Becky coming our way driving
a cow as she approached. There always seemed to be
enough time for Mom to shout, "Billy, here comes Becky."
I knew what this meant for me to do. I would rush out of
the house and race up along the alfalfa path and meet
Becky with her cow. This action on my part would allow
neighbor Becky to retreat to her house and not have to
confront my dad with the intended assignment. I would
turn the cow into the barn yard and inform Dad of the
situation.

I never lingered around much. At my young age, it
did not seem proper to do so. Dad would observe when
the natural events had occurred and would remove the cow
from the barn lot and into my supervision. I was there
waiting outside the lot knowing full well that I had still
another assignment before me. I would drive the cow back
up the path towards Becky's house. Becky would be there
waiting for me to return with her freshly bred cow.

In about nine months, plus or minus a day or two, a
calf would be born to this cow. Becky would call down on

the phone and request that I come up to see her. She would give me a dollar to give to Dad, and she always gave me a quarter for my valuable assistance. What a windfall in cash for me! I had enough to purchase a six-shooter cap gun at Arter's dime store. What a deal!

I do not remember Becky coming to visit us on very many occasions. There must have been some magic gate or line in the dust that she would not cross. Even as young as I was, I knew that she was embarrassed to come face to face with my dad. Mom would go to see her quite often. I recall going along and enjoying the nice cool water that her windmill provided.

Raising Hell and Spreading It

We had some other neighbors I thought were our most interesting couple, named Zeek and Maude. The talk of the neighborhood was that when this couple was first married, they were the sharpest looking and acting couple around. They built a new brick house that had, of all things, a bathroom. This was unheard of in that day. There was no plumbing. But this house was so up to date in planning. The house had been planned to have indoor plumbing at some time. When I lived in this community, they had the same little path to a little outhouse like the rest of the neighbors.

Something happened over the years of blissful occupation of this beautiful home. Things became more and more in disarray in their home. The appearance of the couple went down along with the condition of the buildings. They became more and more open in their arguments to the point that many neighbors witnessed their disagreements.

Zeek's usual appearance was something else. He wore gum boots that always had cow manure on them. He wore the gum boots spring, fall, summer and winter. He always needed a shave. He seemed to always have on more clothing than was needed, particularly in the summertime when it was hot. The things he wore looked as if they would fall off at any moment. He spoke in a rough, deep voice. Maude's appearance coordinated well with his. Her hair hung in strings down around her face. Her dresses dragged on the ground, and she also wore boots. Her boots were of the four buckle arctic type, always unhooked, covered with droppings of chickens or cows. She had a way of pursing her face and lips and frowning and squinting when she talked to you.

One time, another of our neighbors walked in on Zeek when he was standing on top of the kitchen table. Zeek had a crock full of freshly made apple butter in one of his arms. He was using the other hand to smear this wonderful by-product of the apple all over the kitchen walls. The neighbor asked the most natural question, "Zeek, what on earth are you doing?" Zeek responded, "Well, the old lady is raising hell and I'm spreading it." I did not know how she raised hell. I knew how Dad raised pigs. Nobody raised hell around my house. To this very day this couple stands out in my memory as "Gum Boot and Raising Hell." This event was viewed as humorous throughout the neighborhood, but it was an example of the events one might expect to go on in their house.

More About Zeek

Zeek would come up to our house and on many occasions ask to borrow Dad's tools and farm equipment. Some things Dad found convenient to very graciously refuse to lend. But some of the time he simply got caught in the timing and would consent to the lending. Zeek liked to borrow Dad's dump hay rake. I think he did this every time he made hay and that was often through the course of the summer. Zeek would bring his hay wagon with a team hitched to it, and after getting permission to borrow the rake he hooked it to the rear of the wagon. On more than one occasion he would turn a corner too quickly and break a wooden shaft. He was the type of farmer who always carried several pieces of bailing wire with him at all times. On the times that the shaft would break, he would just wire it together with the bailing wire. We had a turn in our driveway by the barn and garden and you could count on old Zeek hitting one of the posts. I got so I would stand by waiting for this to happen. Anything for excitement in those days.

Zeek would bring the rake home in the same way, behind the wagon. After all, he needed a way to ride back home. Zeek walked with a limp from some previous injury not properly taken care of. He would park the rake in the barn yard and go on his way without any comment to Dad. I would hear Dad and Mom talking about this situation and agreeing that Dad should not loan him any more tools. But Dad would go to Akron and get a piece of lumber and fix the rake shaft. He knew all too well that there would be another occasion for loaning the rake back to Zeek. Anyway, Dad wanted the rake to be in good shape for the next time he hooked old Charley back into the shafts.

Dad was well thought of in the neighborhood. Everyone knew that he did not have as many resources to farm as some of the neighbors did. But Dad worked hard and tried his best to keep his equipment in good shape. Broken equipment was like having weeds in the fence row to Dad. Unthinkable.

My first employment outside of the home was for Zeek and Maude. They hired me to drop potatoes at potato planting time. He would hitch up one horse to a single shovel plow and plow a furrowed row. I would fill up a five gallon bucket with pieces of potato cut so that each contained an eye for sprouting. I would walk down the plowed furrow and drop a piece every ten inches or so. I would step on the potato piece so that it would be implanted in the dirt. Zeek would then hitch his horse to a single section of a spike tooth harrow. He would set the harrow to where it was functioning at no more than a drag. He would drive the horse with the harrow cross ways to the rows and this action would fill up the furrow.

The first day of my employment stands out very vividly in my memory. I showed up at twelve noon and worked until six that evening. This was hard work for a twelve year old. I had to almost drag the heavy bucket when I would first start out with it full. When quitting time came, Zeek took me aside and with a big smile, like he was really doing something wonderful, gave me a quarter. I hurried home and the first thing Mom said to me was "Well, how much did they pay you for all of your hard work?" I showed her the quarter. " Billy, tomorrow you must tell them that you must have at least seventy-five cents for a full days work," she said. "Be sure and let them know this before you start to work," Mom added. The first thing I did at six the next morning when reporting to work was to inform Zeek of this instruction from my mom. Immediately Zeek and Maude went into a huddle and, after some grumbling amongst themselves, finally decided they would pay me what my mom had instructed me to ask for.

The word that was out in the neighborhood was not to be caught eating in Maude's kitchen. I would hear tales of the untidiness when I was growing up and would have said I probably would not eat there, either. On prior occasions I had observed her sitting at the kitchen range with her elbow on the edge of the warm part of the stove. I wondered how this could be. I don't remember discussing whether I would eat with them or not. At noontime, all three of us quit the planting and went to the house. I watched her start the lunch. She went to the kitchen table where they usually ate. It was piled high with all sorts of things. I remember her swiping some of the things away and in this process she made room for me.

I can not recall exactly what we had for lunch. I'm sure it contained some sort of potatoes, boiled or whatever. But the fact was that I was impressed with the way the lunch tasted. I went home boasting of this fact. I could say that all of the rumors were not exactly correct.

Zeek often hired me to help him make hay. Some times my job was to pitch the hay onto the wagon. Zeek would receive the loose hay and tramp it down in order to pack on all he could. We needed a minimum of three to do the task properly once we reached the barn. I would stick the fork, Zeek would hire another person to work in the mow and he would drive the team hitched to the hay fork rope.

Early on, I gained a reputation in the neighborhood that I could stick a grapple fork along with the best. The other type of fork used in those days was the harpoon fork. It was the older of the fork types and was slowly disappearing from the hay making scene. The horses pulled the rope that pulled the fork up to the crest of the barn to a carrier positioned on a hay track. The carrier would release and roll along the track until it was over the place in the mow that you wanted it dumped. This was accomplished with a tug on the trip rope hooked to the grapple fork.

Sometimes Zeek would be upset with life. He would give the command for the horses to "getty-up" and, at the same time, he would stick the horses in the back with a pitchfork. The sharp tines of the fork made them respond with a jerk. Zeek's horse harness left much to be desired and would often break. This only made Zeek more upset and his mood went from bad to worse.

At times I would trade off and work in the mow instead of sticking the fork. The job in the mow was to scatter the loose hay about and tramp it down. The more tramping I would do, the more hay could be put into the mow. On some of these occasions when Zeek was yelling at his horses and the harness was breaking and he would get so terribly upset, I would watch through a crack in the barn boards. I thought it to be pretty hilarious.

Zeek had two sons. He favored the oldest and his wife the youngest. This became very evident to me on one occasion. It was another hay making time. I was working in the mow and watched through the cracks in the barn. Zeek's youngest son would not help in the hay making and on this occasion could be seen sitting in the shade of the front porch. Zeek, knowing full well that he had to pay out his good money to me, was not very happy. With the cursing at the horses, and the harness popping loose, it all was really tearing old Zeek up. He would look up towards the porch and cuss up a storm. Then to add more salt to the wound, Maude came out and served lemonade to the youngest son. At this point, Zeek really blew his cork. The phrase that he uttered, and the expression of hate, is very vividly lodged in my memory. "When the God Damn Judgment Day comes, he will get his, he will!" This was very shocking since the expression contained language that was strictly forbidden in a community as heavily churched as ours was. Cursing was not permitted in our house or anywhere around it.

Elections, Bib-Overalls
and Lock the Doors

Politics were fairly open in a small community such as Akron. Most people in the community talked freely of how they felt about various issues. We were not misled or tugged this way or that by the media as happens today. The Akron News only reported who had died or a big fire at someone's barn. A lot of the paper contained ads from the local merchants seeking the business of the community. Current events of what was happening in Washington D.C. or in Indianapolis, our state capital, were almost never an item in the local paper. In our case, even the radio was seldom available. If we had a neighbor who had a good set of batteries and his radio was working, we would sometimes get a national news piece. Farmers might stop and talk about such things across the fence, and the ladies of the neighborhood would sometimes discuss these important matters over the party line. Everyone did not need to be personally called. You could always count on some of them listening in on the party line. No one got shook up about someone listening in. Most of the subscribers did it.

Zeek was a Democrat and Maude was a Republican. The local party leaders would make sure that both of them were driven into Akron to vote on election day. The Democrats would bring a new pair of bib-overalls for Zeek to wear as an added incentive. I can't recall what the Republicans did for Maude. Whoever returned to the house first would lock the doors on the other. Our house would usually get a visit from the one locked out. We could hear them a fussing all of the way up across the fields to our house. The one who got locked out would share tales of dissatisfaction. I would listen in and thought this to be most unusual. Time would pass and both would cool off and before long the doors would be unlocked and life would go on again.

Zeek, More Hay, and Mother Nature

Neighbor Zeek would sometimes need more hay than he had on his farm. He would contract with anyone in the area who had extra to purchase outright all of the hay rights for a specified cutting. On many occasions, Zeek would hire me to help him cut the hay and sometimes rake it, using Dad's rake. More than anything else he would need my help to "make the hay" or bring it into the barn. Often, the fields that he rented were several miles from Zeek's farm and his barn. Since Zeek was somewhat crippled in his hip and leg, he would work on the wagon, load the hay that I would pitch up by hand with a fork. Some of the time he would employ another young man from the neighborhood.

After each wagon full was loaded in the field, we would make the long trip on the state highway to deliver the hay to the barn. I can see us now, all of us sitting up on the wagon load of hay, as the horses trudged along pulling the wagon. Since the trip along the highway would take as much as forty-five minutes, or maybe even an hour, Zeek would have reason to recognize the call of mother nature. When this happened, he simply pulled the team and wagon over on the berm of the road. He would stop the team, get down from the wagon, go to the edge of the

41

berm, drop his bib overalls and proceed to do what mother nature had convinced him he needed to do. When this first happened in my presence, I thought I would die with embarrassment. I would scrunch down in the hay, for fear someone might also recognize me. People in cars were passing up and down the road, and all had easy view of what was going on. I later found it to be somewhat amusing and could manage to come up with a chuckle now and then.

Speaking of Tobacco

One time Dad's pouch of Bagpipe chewing tobacco fell out of his back pocket while he was plowing with the breaking plow. The pocket that it fell out of was directly over the opened furrow. I spent considerable time shoveling through the freshly plowed field searching for his tobacco. I did not find it. Chewing tobacco was one of Dad's luxuries that was a given in our family. When I was big enough to go to town and purchase the groceries from Dan Leininger's General Store, I learned very quickly to say, "A couple Bagpipes, please." The clerks in the store knew what I had asked for and put it in the order. Mother taught us to not begrudge Dad his chewing. "He works hard and a quarter every few days is just fine," she would remind us.

For many years my dad grew his own chewing tobacco. The sight of tobacco growing would sometimes bring curious folk out from town to see what it looked like. Dad had picked up the skill of raising tobacco while growing up in Kentucky. He planted enough to make several twists or at least enough to last him throughout the year. When he cut the stalks he hung them in the corn crib storage area, high up next to the tin roof. The heat from the roof would speed up the drying and curing of the tobacco. In Kentucky they had used barns made especially for the purpose of curing. In some of Dad's after supper stories, he explained the curing process.

A story was told in the neighborhood about a local farmer who chewed home grown tobacco. All of the men that I saw chew twist tobacco would cut off small pieces with their pocket knife and put them into their mouths. Twist tobacco has the stems still in it and they must be removed from the mouth in order to chew the tobacco. The men would usually do this by stripping the stems through an open gap of their teeth. It was not common to see the dentist very often, if ever. When most of the men in the area smiled they exposed a gap in their teeth here and there. If they had any of the twists left, it of course went back into whatever type of pouch they were using.

The setting for this story is a day that the neighborhood men were threshing at one of the neighborhood farms. At dinner time, this thoughtful tobacco chewing farmer did not want to leave any trace of his tobacco in his hostess's spick and span home and left his pouch outside the house. Others had noticed this thoughtful fellow's action and decided to trick him. It was not uncommon to find a nest of young mice on a farm, and so the tricky farmers put a few young mice into their chewing friend's tobacco pouch. After a delicious meal the unwary farmer retrieved his tobacco pouch and proceeded to fill his mouth with the contents. Following his usual custom, he began removing what he thought were tobacco stems from his mouth. The farmer soon discovered that some of the items he was stripping between his teeth were mice feet and tails! Dad said the man became extremely angry, and I can see why!

Another tobacco story concerned our neighbor, Zeek. At one point in his life he chewed tobacco. Zeek did not have a telephone in his home and would walk the short distance to our house to use ours. When chewing tobacco, a lot of spitting is required. One particular day, Zeek was engaged in a long conversation with Hub Stoner, who was the President of the local bank, and he needed to spit. Zeek simply cocked up his arm, and let it fly right down the sleeve of his coat. I thought my mom was going to faint away. Those of us present talked about that incident for years and years.

Steam Engines, Threshing Machines and Water Wagons

Most of the farmers in our area planted several kinds of grain crops. Wheat and oats were generally both planted. When the grain was ripe it was harvested by grain binders in my earlier days. Combines started to come on the scene when I came into my teens. The grain binder cut the grain and then tied it into bundles that were placed in shocks to dry and cure. Cutting and harvesting of grain always happened at the hottest time of summer. The poor horses would get very hot and tired pulling the binder. Dad would have to rest them frequently. He would make a "round" around the field and then he would rest them for a few minutes. When I was old enough, my job was to do the shocking. Up until this time I had been the official water boy. Thistles would get into the grain bundles and prick my hands; we did not have the luxury of leather gloves in those hard times. I learned quickly how to gingerly pick up the bundle and to check very carefully for thistles. Even with such caution, I would always end the day with many scratches and sore hands. I accepted it as what was necessary for the time.

My dad decided to purchase a tractor, and found an old used Fordson. The tractor was not in very good shape. Dad always seemed to be working on it. He only paid seventy five dollars for it, but even that was a lot of money for that time. The wheels had large extension rims to give the tractor more traction so it could stay on top of the ground when it was extremely soft. Dad never took the rims off but would use them everywhere. The first time Dad used the tractor to pull the grain binder he caught the wheat field on fire. The exhaust manifold became cherry red. Dad was not used to such modern equipment and was not watching the grain as it rubbed in and around the hot manifold.

Dad, cutting wheat with a binder and a four horse team.

The grain would stay in shocks for several days. I do not recall exactly just how many. Dad was always the judge of this. He would walk around the field chewing on straws that he would pluck out of the shocks. I guess he knew how dry the straw needed to be.

As soon as Dad would pronounce the grain ready, and if we could get a few rainless days in a row, threshing would begin. Dad would talk to the other neighbors about what they thought of their grain and if they thought it ready or not. The start of threshing was a neighborhood decision. This was an event that the entire community worked on together. Almost everyone shared in the work. Most of the crops were planted at about the same time so maturity of the grain would be about the same. On its own, harvesting grain could be a very big undertaking, but as a neighborhood project it was made much easier.

A man lived in our neighborhood by the name of Charley Rader. Charley owned a threshing machine and he powered it with a large steam engine. He was in touch with the farmers in the neighborhood and knew when to be ready. Someone, probably whoever lived the closest to Charley, started the process. The steam engine and thresher moved very slowly from one farm to another. He would start out with his rig and begin with the closest farm that was ready. Dad knew who he would be helping and who would return the help. I used to get pretty excited when I saw the threshing rig coming down the road, even if I knew it was coming to our farm.

I loved to watch Charley hook the steam engine to the threshing machine and push it up the small incline in front of our barn. He would dig holes in the ground for the rear wheels to fall into. Then he put planks underneath the front wheels to level the machine, as it needed to be level in order to thresh properly. The thresher had a long blower pipe. Charley would guide the blower pipe up into the hay mow as he slowly pushed the thresher in place in front of the barn. This part of the procedure was very exciting. I totally expected Charley to hit the barn. The pipe blew the straw into the mow to be saved for stock bedding during the winter months.

Steam requires water. Water was hauled in a tank wagon to the threshing site from whatever water hole in the area was available. Two horses pulled the water wagon. My brother, Emerson, had this job for at least one season. One time he took me with him and I helped him pump water from a sink hole into the water wagon. The sink holes were certain spots in our neighborhood where water would collect from rains and never leave. The water table would be very close to the top of the ground and so also helped to supply the hole with a good water supply.

You wouldn't think of drinking this water, but it worked just fine for making steam.

All of this preparation was fascinating to me. I watched in amazement as the entire neighborhood of farmers all reacted so alike to the signs and progress of nature. As if performing in a giant chorus, the entire neighborhood had prepared the fields, planted the seeds, watched together the progress, and listened for Charley Rader to announce his approach into our community with a shrill whistle from his steam engine. The sound of the whistle climaxed the need for any more waiting; threshing had begun. This seemed like magic to me.

As Charley placed the threshing machine, the neighbors started to arrive. They knew exactly where to go and start loading. Some of them knew not to bring wagons but just their pitchforks. They would toss the bundles up to the wagon driver who loaded his bundle rack wagon in his own particular way. Sometimes, when I was not tall enough to toss bundles up, I would climb up on the bundle rack in front and drive the team of horses for the owner of the wagon. There were certain ones that I felt comfortable in helping.

The men on the ground would be extremely careful as they pushed over the shock. They would be looking for snakes. Tossing a bundle onto the wagon with a rattlesnake hanging on would create more excitement and danger than we needed. If it did happen, the farmer on the wagon hit the ground running just as soon as he saw the snake. I did witness such an incident, wherein a thoughtless man pitched a snake onto the wagon of a farmer noted for his fear of rattlesnakes. When it happened, the farmer on the wagon came off in a hurry and started chasing the other man around the field with his pitchfork. It was quite a while before he convinced him that he was sorry about what he had done.

Trading labor was a common thing in those days. Dad helped the neighbors when they threshed and they helped us. When I became a teenager and grew strong enough, I found the threshing ring to be a source of earning spending money. I gained a reputation of being a good grain handler. This meant that I could bag the grain or, if the grain was caught loose, I could use the grain shovel with the best of the farmers in the area. Sometimes a farmer would hire me to take his place in helping another farmer. They would always put me to handling the grain. I enjoyed threshing work. The excitement of it all and the cash I could earn was lots of fun.

The expression "she really put on a threshing dinner" had real meaning down on the farm. One of the fun times while I was working on the threshing ring was the noon hour. At each farm that we went to, the lady of the house would try to out-do what the other ones ahead of her had done. It looked to me like the women remembered from year to year what each had served and did their best to do something more spectacular.

When the rig moved to a new location in the afternoon and perhaps had a short amount to thresh, we might have to move again before a noon time rolled around. The lady of that house would simply help out at the next house. I thoroughly enjoyed the meals. These were the days that I could really put the food away. Good cooks were followed by and respected for their reputations. Towards noon, the talk in the field and around the threshing site turned to what we might expect for dinner. Our mouths would start watering for skillet fried chicken, Swiss steak, tender enough to be cut with a fork, chocolate meringue pie and fresh peach cobbler. Lunch would be too skimpy for a noontime meal. Lunch was what you carried to school.

The Cussing Neighbor

We had one neighbor who had a reputation of not being able to carry on a conversation without cursing almost every other word. I am sure there were times when it seemed like every word from his mouth was a swear word. This neighbor very seldom came into our house. He would knock on the back door and talk through the screen door. There must have been something about my mom and her ability to listen that kept this man knocking at the door. Sometimes Dad would be in the house, but most of the time it would be my mom who had to listen to his swearing. I would hide behind her, peeking out from behind the stove or some other piece of furniture. To me, it was great sport to hear all of those words that were forbidden in our household. Whenever he had a tale of woe to spin, I believe he came by to tell it to Mom.

I recall one of his tales quite vividly. "Mrs. Shrout," he said (he always called her Mrs. Shrout) "all hell broke loose yesterday. You can't believe what a damn day I had. Two of my cows had calves yesterday. One of the calves was born without an asshole. I tried to make one for it and the son-of-a-bitch bled to death. The other God damn calf was born with the scours and he shit himself to death." My little ears were really humming while hearing all of this pour out. My mom would swallow hard, and I know was saying silent prayers for the good Lord to give her strength and wisdom in how to respond to this man. Mom would keep her composure and always respond in some way that kept him coming back to tell yet another tale of woe.

A tragic ending came to this cussing neighbor. Neighborhood talk was that he had started going to church and was converted. All of the neighbors were happy and proud for him. In his efforts to stop cursing, he decided that he could not change. His wife found him in the barn on a Sunday morning, dead. He had hung himself with the hay rope.

My First Celery

There was a small farmhouse located about a quarter of a mile east of the Shewman farm house that we referred to as the "little brown house." Various tenants lived there while I resided at the Shewman farm. One such person was named Mike. He lived there with his wife and two children.

The entire farm that went with the brown house was in muck. The property bordered Mud Lake, a small fishing lake surrounded by this and other farms in the area. Mike was a good muck farmer and enjoyed working in the muck. He could always produce good looking onions and potatoes. I was visiting him with my dad one day when I noticed a strange looking stalk-type plant growing. The stalk was covered with tar paper and was about a foot tall and was growing in bunches. Mike told us that this plant was called celery and that the paper staked next to it was to bleach the stalks. In those days celery was sold bleached and not sold green as it is today. I thought that it went very well with my gravy bread.

Windmills and Cool Water

I thought the best tasting water came from windmills. Several of the neighbors had them. I think everyone had one but us. The windmills were allowed to run a great deal of the time. They could be tied off or hooked in such a fashion that the wheel could spin but the working part of the pump would stand idle. Sometimes only a small stream of water would be coming out. The size of the stream depended on how hard the wind was blowing and how fast the plunger was going up and down. One of the good tasting windmill-driven wells belonged to Rube and Nerly Royer. One of my field assignments was to keep the water jug full. I would go over to their place when working in any of the north fields carrying with me my empty water jug with a corn cob stopper.

It seems like only yesterday that I was standing in front of the screen door knocking. The Royers had a screened-in porch that I always thought to be very neat. There were lots of mosquitoes in that part of Indiana and a screened-in porch was pretty nice. Nerly would come to the door and take my jug and fill it from the windmill inside the porch. I would always stand on the outside and never go into the porch. She would ask about Mom and if she were feeling well. Nerly always wore a large bonnet and would sometimes have it on even though she was in the shade of the porch. Perhaps when I found her like this she had just come in from the outside where the sun had been shining.

The water from neighbor Becky's windmill-driven well was also good. The longer water is pumped, the cooler it becomes. Sometimes the windmill would pump for hours. At our house, we pumped by hand and this meant that it would not be very cold.

Other Thirsty Experiences

About a mile south of us lived George and Bessie Kreig. I liked to work for George when he made hay and needed help. Bessie was a neighbor lady that I remember my mom talking with a lot. They would talk over the party line for great lengths of time. Someone would jiggle the receiver up and down at their home signaling that they wanted the line. In doing this, without saying an audible word, they could register their disfavor of Mom and Bessie tying up the line for so long. We even went to their house as dinner guests a couple of times. They went to the same church as we did and they kept up with my progress in growing, and when they thought I was big enough, they hired me to help them make hay.

George was another one of those frugal farmers who patched his horse's harness with most anything he could lay his hands on. George was also likely to yell at the horses and sometimes use the sharp end of the pitch fork to make his point with them. He was the only neighbor that I knew of who used slings to take in hay. A sling was made out of rope and wooden one by twos as wide as the wagon bed. They resembled a type of net. The first sling was placed on the floor of the hay wagon. George owned a hay loader. The loader was attached to the rear of the wagon and as the wind row of hay was straddled the loader fed the hay up and onto the wagon. Two people could work this function very nicely. George and I made a lot of hay just between the two of us.

We would tramp the hay down as firmly as we could and after it was two feet in depth we would spread out another sling. After we had four slings of hay we would unhook the loader from the wagon and go to the barn with the load of hay. The slings were pulled up into the mow in a similar fashion as in the grapple fork method.

In George's operation, I had the hard job of working the mow. Untangling the hay from the sling was very difficult. George told me that during the winter it was even more difficult to remove the hay from the mow to feed. It really became tangled up as I would push it in and about the mow area. When all four slings had been deposited into the mow we would hang the empty slings on the front of the hay rack of the wagon and proceed back to the field for another load.

One of the more memorable events that happened as we progressed through the day was in the consumption of lemonade. On the way to the barn with the full load of hay we would pass by the house. We would always stop at the house before unloading and as a reward for our hot, sweaty efforts in the field we would receive all of the lemonade we could drink. That was the best tasting lemonade I have ever had. Bessie would not put ice in it but depended on the windmill to provide the very cool water and besides that, she knew how to make great lemonade. My mind would be occupied with thoughts of the next glass of that most delicious delicacy. While loading the wagon I would dream up a storm about the pleasant experience waiting for us. Then after we unloaded the hay in the barn, we would again stop by the house on our way back to the field.

George knew exactly what he was doing. He had me right where he wanted me. I was his captive. I would work feverishly loading the wagon in the field. When I was at the barn I would see how quick I could get the hay put in the mow. I loved that lemonade! I have often wondered how much of that sweet lemony drink I consumed during a work day.

I happened to be in Akron many years later and stopped at Bessie's estate sale. There on the table waiting to be auctioned was the lemon squeezer she had so skillfully used. I was successful in bidding on it and have it among my prized souvenirs.

Blow the Bugle, George

For a couple of years I rode to church with the Kreigs. They drove a '35 Pontiac and always went to church on Sunday. I would get all cleaned up and put on the best that I had and waited for the sound of their car horn. When I heard the horn I would run out to the highway and get into the front seat with George. Bessie would be in the back seat and we would proceed towards Akron. Arrangements had also been made to pick up another lady on the way to church. I always thought it humorous to hear Bessie say as we approached the other rider's house, "Blow the bugle, George." George would always obey with a long blast on the ol' Pontiac horn.

3

LITTLE
BILLY GOES TO
SCHOOL

Dad Gets Up

The first thing that Dad would do on a cold winter morning would be to arise, sometimes as early as three o'clock and go to the cold living room. The fire in the old Ray-Boy stove would have long before gone out and the room and all of the house for that matter could very well be around or even below zero. Dad would hurry to build a fresh fire in the stove. He would pull a straight chair up close, reverse the position of the chair and sort of straddle the chair, placing his head on his arms between the knobs that were at the top of the chair back. He would snooze in this position until about five or five-thirty. By this time the stove's inner jacket would be cherry red and the intense heat would awaken him. Then Dad would go to the kitchen and start a fire in the kitchen range.

On the real cold nights my mother would put the water bucket on the reservoir end of the kitchen range. If someone needed a drink, during the night it would probably not be frozen. On some mornings, this part of the house would be so cold that water did indeed freeze in the water bucket while sitting on the kitchen range. Dad would light the small coal oil lantern and suit up for the exit to the cold Indiana morning. On the mornings that there was a lot snow, Dad would wrap gunny sacks around his pant legs and tie them off with binder twine. This procedure kept the snow in the large drifts from getting his pant legs wet. My dad could always make do. Out he would go, trudging through the deep snow, swinging his little lantern to light his way even though he knew the path by heart. In all too short a time I would be following the path he had made through that cold Indiana morning.

The Rest of Us Get Up

Dad's departure to the barn was to be the wake up signal for my mother. One of the first chores she did was to call up the stairs to my older brothers. Those that were still living at home needed to know that it was morning and their dad was expecting them to come to the barn and help him with the morning milking. When I was about ten years old, I was called to help with the milking. My mother's call then became the start of the cold winter days in my life on the farm.

I recall very vividly those cold mornings. The cold air was able to reach through the tons of clothes that I managed to struggle into. In getting up, I would push back as many as four comforters and swing my bare feet out onto the ice cold linoleum floor. I did not linger long at this point. I hurriedly donned the inner layer of clothes I had left on the edge of the bed from the night before. The temperature in my bedroom would sometimes get down to below zero. Snow would often drift in through the cracks around the old fashioned, single-paned windows. I usually took time to shake off the snow that drifted onto my blankets. There were so many comforters on my bed that my body heat did not have a chance to melt the snow that landed on them.

63

Down the stairs I would go in the dark of early morning. I would put on my heaviest work coats. I usually had some tall boots or four buckle arctics to put on. I did not dress as warm as my Dad in that I did not wrap gunny sacks around my legs. I also did not spend as much time as Dad did outside in all of the cold weather. Dad would have to get the milking equipment ready and then do all of the morning feeding. I just had to do my share of milking the cows.

After the milking was completed, we all came in to the toasty warm kitchen and partook of the breakfast that mother had prepared. Sometimes we would have sausage patties, fried eggs, and biscuits or in later years "light bread" from the local bread man who delivered it to the door. They were wonderful yet simple meals. There was not too much variety in what Mother could fix for us to eat. Today when I let my mind wander back to that cozy kitchen, I realize that I go out and eat the same food today and pay several dollars for the privilege.

Before breakfast I would throw a little water on my face and make a small attempt to wash the cow off of my hands. Later I would change to my one and only set of school clothes, a pair of corduroys and a flannel shirt. I remember well the high top shoes I used to lace up. There was a pocket on the side of one shoe and I could place a small pocket knife in it. A knife usually came with each new pair of shoes purchased. All of my clothes and shoes were purchased at the Dan Leininger and Sons General Store.

Then it would be time to start watching for the school hack. As we became a little more fancy in later years, we called it the school bus. There was an east window in my parent's bedroom that looked directly out towards the little county road where the bus would be making its approach to our house. When we first saw the bus stop at the "little brown house" just east of our place, we knew it was time to leave the house, and go down the hill to the county road.

The School Hack

I remember one particular day in late August of 1932. My mother told me to go out and watch for Don Morris, my first school bus driver. She told me that she had seen him go into town and he would be coming back soon. He lived below us on the road and would pass right in front of our house. She told me to look "ol' number nine"

Roy (Tommy) Miller, and good 'ol' number nine school hack

over real good. She wanted me to become familiar with what the bus looked like from the outside. When I would be coming out of the school house the buses might all look alike to a little boy who never got around much.

Mom knew that in a few days school would be starting. This might be the only chance I would get to practice recognizing the bus that I should get on to come home. Sure enough, it went by and I did what I was told to do. I looked the bus over and felt that I would be very capable of finding the right one when it came time to do so. I remember the bus was made out of wood. It would look very crude today. Roy Miller drove for the next eleven years.

We rode that bus to school each day. We were the last ones to get on the bus. Some of the kids were on it for almost an hour. It would start its pick up south and west of Disco, a small community about three miles south of our farm. The bus would weave its way back and forth up and down the country roads and make its general approach to the school in Akron. By the time the bus got to our place, there was not much room left. In fact, I can remember the times that my oldest brother attending school would have to sit on a folding camp stool in the doorway.

I remember, all too well, the mornings that I, as the smallest child, would have to sit on the middle seat made of an eight inch padded plank running down the middle of the bus. On each side, a row of seats with the backs to the outside of the bus, faced the middle and the little short row that I sat on. On a a lot of those cold mornings I would have to sit with my little nose at about the same height as some of the bigger farm boys arctic buckle boots, fresh from the cow barn and with all of the pungent aroma that the boots had managed to garner.

It would only take about ten minutes to get to the Akron Grade School. Akron was and still is a little town of fewer than one thousand residents. We were taken to the grade school first. After that the older students from the seventh grade through high school were taken to the high school building.

Akron Grade School

Both the grade and high school buildings are long gone, but their memories stand out in my mind as though they just happened. The grade school building was made out of brick and was placed in the middle of a block square piece of land. A set of railroad tracks was on one side of the property and a Brethren Church was across the street. Houses and vacant lots were on the other streets.

The school building had two levels plus the basement. Eight classrooms were on the two main levels. In the basement was a large playroom, two restrooms and of course the furnace room. We would use the playroom a lot in the winter when it was too cold to go outside to play. We would get in the middle of the playroom at recess and the boys would wrestle up a storm. It seemed that young lads of the early grades and in that particular time span always wanted to flex their muscles. We must have gone home looking like a real mess.

The building had old wood floors that were so oil soaked that they must have been a real fire hazard. At one time the school tried out a hot lunch program and the playroom was the dining room. I think it cost about three cents for lunch.

69

Ashes, Pennies and Mary Biek

Early memories of grade school bring me to mind of my going down to the furnace room and offering my services to a janitor by the name of Lew Wade. Mr. Wade would pay another boy and me a penny a tub to carry ashes to the outside and put them on a huge pile that collected as the school year progressed. This was a job that needed our attention about two times a week, so the other lad and I would have about two cents each to do with what we pleased.

I would take my two cents and hurry over across the street north of the grade school. Since we were not allowed to use the main streets, I would dash through the empty lot behind Mary Biek's little home-run store. She used the front or living room of her house to stock things the neighbors might run out of, such as bread and milk, and some of the little sweet things that were popular at that time. My certain interests rested in the penny candies that she had displayed in her show case.

If I needed a new lead pencil for school, I would sometimes save my pennies until I had three, enough to purchase a striped pencil. The penny pencils were easily recognized with their flat wood finish and the cheap looking

70

pointed eraser on top. If your pencil was of the multi-color variety, that might indicate that your family had some material means. I do not recall having a lot of concern for other fineries, but I was somewhat concerned about the kind of pencil that I used. I am sure that a lot of the children in school with me were not much better off in worldly goods and perhaps suffered the same kind of reaction, if not to pencils then to something else.

Baloney, Paper Bags and The Rich

Another possible test of your financial place or position in the ladder of life was in the kind of lunch that you carried and how you carried it. My parents could not afford to go to Dan Leininger's General Store and purchase baloney or other prepared lunch meats. The more affluent were able to purchase not only store bought meats but also nice neat looking Kraft paper lunch bags to carry their lunches in. A lot of the kids would throw away the paper bag and bring a fresh new one the next day.

Once in a while my mother, knowing the importance of this demonstration of ladder positioning, would come

71

across a paper bag and would smooth it out nice and neat and pack my lunch in it. When I had finished eating lunch I would make sure no one was watching and I would again smooth the bag out and skillfully sneak it home for use again the next day.

Most of the time my lunch was wrapped in some old newspaper that Mom was able to locate either from a neighbor or sometimes from my married sister, Verna, who usually took a daily newspaper. We had to collect the newspapers because the only newspaper that I remember coming into the house was the Akron News. It was a very small paper and there were times even it did not show up at our house. Hard times might mean the one dollar for a year's subscription was just too much and had to be used elsewhere.

There never seemed to be a piece of white string to tie around the newspaper, so Mom would use some of her black thread from her sewing supplies. I used to think this looked very cheap and I guess it bothered me some. We never could afford a daily newspaper, or at least that is what my dad had convinced us. On the newspaper lunch days I would try to hide my lunch as I sat at my desk and ate it. On the days I had a nice paper bag I would flaunt it while eating with the rest of the class.

John, His Balloon Tire Bike
and Sidewalks

The first balloon-tire bike that I rode belonged to a classmate by the name of John Hand. A balloon-tire is about two and one half inches wide. Compared to a high-pressure tire, the balloon tire bike was like riding on air. John was one of the few who had a balloon-tire bike. He lived close to the grade school and would ride his bike to school on some days. I shall always be thankful to John for allowing me to ride his nice, shiny new bike.

There was a sidewalk in front of the grade school building and this made bike riding a new experience for me. I was used to the gravel roads out around the farm and to all of the trouble the loose gravel caused me in my riding efforts. Couple this gravel determent with the fact that my bike was a skinny high pressure tire bike, and there really was a difference riding John's. To be able to ride a balloon-tire bike on a sidewalk and feel like floating on air was a real thrill.

I suppose that is why I still have that pleasant memory with me today. Through the years, I have thought about John and his willingness to let me ride his new bike. How nice of John to do this.

The School Clock

I remember the old school clocks. There was a clock for each room. It seemed that so much of what went on in the school was connected to that particular series of clocks. Sometimes, even today, I catch myself thinking about those clocks and wondering if it will soon be time for recess. Recess meant fifteen minutes of play. In good weather, that could mean playing softball or baseball. We had plenty of time to make a few "outs" in those short fifteen minute periods. We would simply continue the game from one play period to another.

In those days, we had but one method of choosing sides. Usually two of the older or bigger boys would decide that they were in charge and would be the team captains. The rest of us would stand around and wait for them to go through the age-old ritual of using the baseball bat to decide who got to choose the first team mate. They would use the bat and do the hand over hand routine. If you ran out of hand space, you would use the first two fingers of your hand to make a scissor type grip on the bat. If one of the captains decided he could not get a good enough grip on the bat to throw it he would pass, and the one holding the bat would attempt to throw the bat over his shoulder at least ten feet. Success at this feat allowed him to have the first choice of the rest of us potential team mates, who just stood around watching all of the proceedings.

We had another good reason to watch the school clock; that was to know when to eat lunch. The boys would use all haste in consuming their lunches and race out to the school yard to continue the on going ball game.

We also were interested in keeping an eye on the clock to make sure we were ready for "hack time." To those of us who lived in the country, it meant going home and reuniting with our families. A warm and caring atmosphere always seemed to be prevalent in an Indiana farm setting in those days. I would be anxious to tell Mom and Dad about what I had studied that day and to share with my older brothers and sister how truly smart their little brother was becoming. I knew a family closeness then that I do not see many families act out or even talk about today.

One of my older brothers' routines when arriving home from school was to raid the kitchen stove warming closets. Mom put left-overs from what she had prepared for Dad that day in one or both of the warming closets, shelves with doors that were in the South Bend kitchen wood range. If there were some pieces of cornbread, they would fight for possession and then find a raw onion and head to the barn to do chores, eating away on this delicious repast of simple Depression era food. This small snack seemed to to be sufficient to hold over the appetites of hungry growing boys until chores were completed and we could once again gather around the large kitchen table for some of Mom's delightfully tasty supper.

It seemed that no matter how slim the pickings were for items of food, our mom had a way of making the simple, and perhaps short supply, taste as good as that on the tables of the more affluent.

Miss Nellie and the First Grade

I recall very well the first grade in school. On those first days of school, I did not want to come back into the classroom after being outside for recess. I must have been very bashful. I can remember Miss Nellie, the teacher, would come out and persuade me to let her lead me back to the room. I can see myself to this day, hanging back and holding onto the flag pole in the school yard. The pole was situated not too many feet from the front door at the school. All of the other children would scurry back into the building when the bell rang. I would stand there and hang onto the pole and not want to return as I watched the others go by. I think that this only happened a very few times, whereupon I soon became oriented to school procedure.

Miss Nellie and the first grade class.
Author is on left end of the back row.

Miss Nellie was a single teacher at that time. She later married a high school principal. The year I started first grade, there were over sixty anxious youngsters eligible to go into the first grade. The principal, Mr. Fox decided to make two classes, but, there was only one first grade class room. Mr. Fox, decided that he would forgo the use of his office and make that room available for my section of the first grade.

I will always remember the large rope that hung down from the ceiling. The rope was attached to a large clapper type bell that hung high up in the belfry. There was no electric bell in the building. The principal pulled on the rope and rang the bell to notify the students of the start of recess or the noon hour. He also rang the bell to let us know when it was time to come back to our rooms.

The biggest boy in my class was Ray Bradway. Ray stood a full head taller than I. He had an adventurous spirit about him. There were times that he was encouraged to pull the rope and ring the bell when Miss Nellie would leave the room. I believe Mr. Fox attended to his misconduct. Mr. Fox would not easily forget such an action. He was principal for several years and, in fact, taught me arithmetic in the fifth and sixth grades.

One day Miss Nellie made a small paper box. She put a slot in the top. Every time anyone of us said the contraction "can't," she would insist that we write our name on a slip of paper and place it in the "can't box." We were taught very early to take a positive position in life. It has been sixty-three years as of this writing, but I can still see the little box that rested upon a small table, on the right front side of the classroom. I like to think that Miss Nellie and her "can't box" made a major contribution towards my attitudes throughout life.

Miss Nellie had a big, gentle, sweet smile that always seemed to be on her friendly face. I have a lot of pleasant memories, thinking back to the stories of the foxes and the Peter Rabbits.

Along about this time, my mom would read to me from library books that my sister, Christeen, would check out on her library card. There was a series of books that dealt with animals and birds with human names. I began to think that the animals and birds were real. Mom, despite her limited education and reading ability, knew how to put the right inflections in her voice. She made the stories come to life. She convinced me that Blacky the Crow and Sammy Bluejay really were cousins and that Peter and Mopsy Cottontail were husband and wife and managed to raise some little babies in some ingenious way.

I looked forward with much anticipation to the times that I would sit on the floor at her knee listening to her masterful way in weaving the animal and bird tales. Most of the happy times were in front of the north kitchen window. It seems a lot of things over the years took place in front of the north kitchen window. This is the spot where Mom would sit with her apron fanned out and count the small amount of change she had dumped into her apron from her egg money jar. Sometimes I had the good fortune of receiving as much as a nickel, if she felt she had enough funds.

Tops, Yo-Yos and Hair

I became involved in the top and yo-yo craze that was very prevalent when I was in grade school. We had one game that we called "keep the pot boiling." All of the boys in my class had a top. They were not too difficult to come by. We tried to keep at least one top spinning at all times. We got to be pretty fancy in some of the tricks we could pull off. The old wooden floors were very rough and had large cracks between the boards, which made it very difficult to keep a top spinning.

When it came to yo-yo spinning, my best memories are of some very aggravating stunts we pulled on the girls of the school. I can still see the boys, and yours truly among them, leaning over the upstairs railing and spinning our yo-yos down in an attempt to catch a girl's hair as she walked up the stairs. What a mess when one of the boys connected their yo-yo and a girl's head of hair. I do not remember ever getting caught in this act, but I'm sure some did.

Martha and Me
and the Four Dollar Cornet

When I was in the first grade, Miss Nellie our teacher, decided that we should try our first endeavor in drama. I can still see it so plainly. We acted out George and Martha Washington. There were four couples. My partner, Martha, was really Jolene Harper. We wore authentic outfits, including wigs. We did all sorts of curtsies and dips and bows. This sort of thing did not meet with much approval by me in those days.

After I became involved I did not seem to know how to get out of it. We did one performance for the high school. Then they wanted me to do it again. I will always remember the way I got out of performing. I came up with the bright idea that if I had a note from my mother saying no more performances, that it might work. After all, I had seen my mother write her name many times and I was pretty sure I could duplicate her handwriting. I wrote the note and signed her name. I gave the note to Miss Nellie. Sure enough, Miss Nellie excused me from further performances. I do not believe that I ever told my mom about this daring act of forgery.

The George Washington Play.
The book's author is the first George on the left.

When I was in the fourth grade, the music teacher that taught both the grade and the high school had try outs at the grade school for new and promising band students. The idea sounded pretty good to me. I remember going down to the first floor of the building to the room that was used just for band and choir or choral classes. Reba Woods was the teacher. She gave me a trumpet and showed me some of the basic things I would need to know. Surprising all of us, I managed to get the horn to work. If you have never blown a trumpet before, it can be difficult.

Miss Woods sent a note home with me that said that in her best judgment little Billy had some possibilities. She thought I could master the trumpet or cornet. Now, money was hard to get in those Depression times, and a new trumpet from Sears catalog would cost around twenty-five dollars. Dad said no way, just a waste of money he didn't have. I thought that this would be it and I would not be able to play in the grade school band. Mom suggested we find out if Miss Woods could locate a used horn.

Well, Miss Woods did find a used cornet. The price was four dollars. Now, where was I to get four dollars? This was early fall and potato harvesting time. I remember picking up potatoes for Albert Bammerlin at three cents a bushel to save up the four dollars. I hurried the funds to Miss Woods, and she was so excited to have me play.

The very first day of using the cornet, the valves stuck. Now what was I to do? I had picked a lot of potatoes for this horn and I sure wanted to play in the band. I brought the cornet home and told Mom my tale of woe.

When Dad came in from doing the milking and evening chores and a good tasting supper was history, Mom made the presentation of my situation with the horn. Dad said, "Bring it to me, I'll take a look at it." I did and, sure enough, Dad, in another of his miracle ways of dealing with a problem with nothing, came up with a solution.

Dad in those days would take a spoon full of Vaseline twice daily. This was supposed to help keep him regular in the daily trips to the three-holer. The local Standard Oil route driver, Walter Harris, had Dad on his list of clients. We did not have a tractor or need gasoline but Dad sure used his share of Vaseline. Dad knew very well what Vaseline did to his inner parts. Dad figured out that maybe the valves, would work much better with a little Vaseline smoothed on them. He kept working with them and finally they broke free and never stuck again after that.

I managed to make some good sounds on the cornet and played along with the rest of the students in the simple pieces that we were given. Miss Woods talked to my brother, Irvin, at the high school building and wanted to know if there was any chance that Billy could have a new trumpet. Irvin talked to Dad and Mom about it that evening, but of course Dad was firm and the discussion was short. Thinking back, I am sure Dad was right. It was very difficult to make ends meet with such a large family and only getting a portion of the crop earnings.

Many of the instruments would freeze up while riding to school on the school bus on some of those cold Indiana mornings. Ray Bradway played the big tuba. I can see that big old horn sitting on top of a steam radiator quite vividly in my memory. It did not take long for his tuba to thaw there and Ray would join the rest of us. The band must have sounded pretty squeaky to anyone listening in.

Some of our band went on to play in the high school band. Others of us knew that we had to accept our financial position in life and yield to the inevitable aftermath of the Great Depression and its shortfalls. It did not seem to me that I could continue at the high school building with any degree of competition using a four dollar cornet. I am sure Miss Woods understood my situation and was probably glad that I did not try it.

4

PETS and OTHER
CRITTERS

The Crows That Did Not Talk

One of my older brothers, Adrian, spent lots of time in the south end of the huckleberry swamp. He seemed to enjoy studying the life of birds and other of nature's creatures. I recall one of our neighbors who knew of Adrian's spending so much time in the swamp referring to my brother as the Swamp Angel. On one occasion, Adrian found some young crows in a nest. They looked full grown but had not flown off the nest. He brought several of the young crows home and put them in the granary building.

He built some pens for them and started to feed them with some of the chicken mash that Dad had purchased, or in some cases, had made from the grain he had raised. In any event, the mash was worth something and in the hard times of the Depression, Dad was not too happy about my brother feeding the mash to a farmer's archenemy.

Adrian read a lot and had read that if you were to split the young crow's tongue, it could be taught to talk. He did not get the opportunity to do any tongue splitting. On one occasion early on in this event, Dad came into the granary. The crows, thinking the person entering the building was my brother, the one who would feed them, opened their mouths and began letting my dad know that they were hungry.

Dad by this time had had enough of this foolishness. He knew that as wild critters, they would wait until the corn he had planted started to sprout and they would pull it up. My dad chewed tobacco. His mouth was supplied with tobacco juice at almost any time. Dad took advantage of this wonderful opportunity to deposit some of the excess juice down the beaks and into the throats of the pleading young crows.

Adrian did not get to find out if the crows would talk. Some of them died and he had to get rid of the rest. Although it might sound cruel, a farmer sometimes had to be cruel to protect his crops.

As I grew up, I also had lots of fun exploring this same swamp and woods area. I saw more crows nests, but I knew better than to try my brother's scheme another time. One time Dad and I shot another batch of young crows from the nest and hung them in the corn fields as decoys to deter other crows from entering the field. This was another one of my dad's make-do ways of dealing with an age old fact of nature.

We always kept our ears tuned to the sounds of summer. I believe Mom and I could hear crows cawing from one end of the Shewman farm to the other. By the time I was about eight years old, I would be detailed out with the twenty gauge shotgun to fire a few shots when we heard the crows flying over, heading for one of our cornfields.

I thought this a big sport and longed to get a big black crow in my sights. It never did happen that way. Shooting them out of the tree was as close as I got to the real sport.

More About My Dogs

Every small lad growing up should have the pleasure of owning a dog. I do not recall any days that I lived on the Shewman farm that I did not have a dog. Everyone in the neighborhood had a dog. Our neighbors, the Royers, had a dog named Tutie. On one occasion, Tutie had a litter of pups and I got one of them. As I remember, this litter of pups was of the Heinz 57 variety. I named my little female pup Patsy. Patsy was a very smart dog. She would stand by the heating stove on a cold morning. She would look up at the stove and then up toward my dad and whine. Even Dad succumbed to this little dog's charms and would pick her up and hold her out over the top of the nice warm stove. Of course Patsy really loved it and attempted to show her gratitude to my dad.

When I was about nine years old my brother, Irvin, talked Dad and Mom into buying a full blooded shepherd pup. Dad gave up five dollars of hard-earned money to purchase this special dog. Shepherds had a reputation of being very trainable to attending for cows in their driving to and from pasture. We decided that as good a name as any for this delightful pup would be Shep.

Shep grew to full size in short time and became well aware of what a farmer expected him to do in tending to cows. He was good. We were all proud of him and his abilities.

One day in early spring, I was helping Dad fix a fence along the county road just north of the barn, just across the road from Becky Hiveley's barn. Shep was about a year old at this time. You could always find him close to me, or wherever Dad was.

Shep number one. He was hit by a truck and killed.

Shep and I went back to the barn for something Dad wanted. When we returned we were on the edge of the county road close to where Dad was repairing fence. Out of seemingly nowhere came a truck driven by S.A. Renaker, who had a regular route of picking up cases of eggs from farmers in the area. I just barely got out of the way myself when the truck hit Shep. He died instantly. I was in a state of shock. Dad said, " Go to the house, Billy, and get a long-handled shovel." For some reason he had not brought one with him for fence repair. The memory of my mom and me walking across the alfalfa field will stay with me all of my life. I can see us hand in hand, me dragging the heavy shovel and both of us crying our hearts out.

Certain events in one's life stand out so much more than others. This was one such memorable event. Mom and I made it to the scene of the accident and I watched my dad bury one of my favorite pets.

Almost immediately after the death of Shep, a stray dog showed up on the farm. It was very common in those days that if you had a dog you no longer wanted you loaded him into your car and hauled him to another neighborhood and dumped him out. This must have been one such critter. He was mostly Collie and was very thin and hungry. I begged Dad to keep the dog and he said I could.

92

With the memory of my recent Shep dog on my mind, I elected to call this stray dog Shep, too.

Shep number two did not possess very much training in cattle attending. Most of the time he only added a great deal of confusion by barking at the wrong end of the cow. He did other odd things, as well. When Dad would start the gasoline engine to pump water for the livestock, the John Deere engine would back-fire loudly as it exhausted its system of running. As the engine cracked loudly many times during the course of adding cool fresh water to the horse tank, old Shep would run around the garden fence barking up a storm.

Shep was with us for a very long time and he continued this running and barking routine each and every time Dad started up the gasoline engine. Heavy grass sod could be found all around the garden fence. Shep ran it so many times that he wore a path deep into the sod and even had it banked at the turns like a race track.

I remember playing a trick on old Shep. I tied binder twine between the garden fence and a cottonwood tree that stood about four feet out from the fence at one of the corners. The very next time Dad started up the engine, I was out in the yard waiting for the action and anticipating much fun in the anticipated excitement.

93

Sure enough, just as soon as the engine started its usual popping and cracking, old Shep started his routine. I had placed the twine at the third corner of his route around the garden, wanting him to be able to get up to full speed before approaching my ingeniously contrived obstacle. Shep did not fail me. He was really laying it down on the back stretch and was concentrating on leaning into the turn as he approached corner number three. Shep hit the several strands of binder twine hard and ended up in a yipping heap almost at my feet. I rolled in the yard, laughing at his plight, but Mother, who had heard all of the commotion, did not think it too funny and let me know so.

Shep liked to chase cars and bark at them. If he could convince them that he was in their path and get the driver of the car to slow up for fear of running over him, Shep thought that he had accomplished something. He would attempt to bite the tires of the car. I have no way of knowing just what he thought he was going to do if he was successful in getting his teeth into a tire. There came that time when he was able to get his mouth and teeth into a tire. For some reason, a friend of the family had driven back into the pasture field, perhaps to gather some peat moss for their yard. The car had stopped for one of us to open a gate. Shep was barking and grabbing at the rear tires as usual. He managed to get hold of one of the tires.

As the car moved ever so very slowly forward through the gate, I saw him hang onto the tire and go around with the tire and have it stop on his mouth. I screamed and yelled to the driver of the tragedy at hand. As soon as we could release his mouth, old Shep ran as fast as he could to the barn. He crawled under the barn and all of us assumed that he would probably die.

In a few days we noticed our old stray dog out in the barn yard limping around but not barking too much. He soon healed and began his endless routines again. About a year after this event, Dad grew tired of his barking and confusion and he hauled him off about five miles distant and let him out of the car. This did not bother old Shep. He found his way home easily. On other occasions, I saw my dad merely shoot or otherwise eliminate undesirable critters, but Dad had a soft spot for Shep and could not just do away with him. Dad was not unlike other farmers of the area. A dog must serve a productive purpose if it were to remain on the farm and be fed.

My brother, Emerson, noticed the situation and while visiting one weekend put Shep into his car. He dropped him off about fifty miles away on his way home. We never saw old Shep again.

All Those Cats

We had so many cats and litters of kittens that one could count them by the dozens at certain times. Sometimes, the mother cat would deposit her young ones on the step just outside the kitchen door. I recall on more than one occasion, that my dad would go out in the dark, not see the kittens, and step right into the middle of the litter. We would hear a lot of screeching and howling but would not think too much about it. When morning came, Dad would usually be the first one out the door and he would clean up the mess.

If something like this happened today the family would go into shock, but it was a perfectly natural accident in those days. After all, we were taught to fret not; behold, more would come along shortly to replace any losses. And sure enough they did.

Milking machines had not arrived on the scene and cows were milked by hand. I can see myself now, squirting milk from the cow's teat across the gutter. About four or five feet away, a cat would be standing poised on its hind feet, waiting for the warm milk to land in its mouth. I only did this when Dad was down at the far end of the milking parlor and could not see what was going on.

Dad would not have appreciated such a waste of a salable product on a critter like a cat, but I noticed that every so often Dad would pour some milk in a pan for the cats. I got to be pretty fancy with my milk squirting and putting my cats through a lot of funny tricks.

Whenever the cat population seemed to get out of control or Dad would have his fill of stepping on kittens on the kitchen step, he would take drastic steps. Down to the swamp he would go with a sack of kittens from some new litter he had noticed when choring at the barn.

On one of these occasions when my curiosity had peaked to its maximum, I went with him. I never went again, for what I saw Dad do lasted me for the rest of my days on the farm. I observed that Dad, with his powerful pitching arm and the assistance of the available tree trunks in the swamp, would quickly bring a smaller cat population to the Shewman farm.

I would give some of the cats names. I always had favorites. I can remember naming one Mickey and another Minnie. It seemed to me that popular mouse names could also be appropriate for cats.

I recall naming one of my favorites Felix. Was I ever surprised one day to find Felix with a litter of kittens. Young farm boys pride themselves in having all kinds of know-how in determining the sex of animals. After all, it was a common occurrence for us and we thought we knew all there was to know in that category. Felix had used the straw that surrounded the water tank in the well house to make the first home for her litter. She soon moved them to another location.

It seemed that all of my mother cats were moving their families from one place to another. We had so much kitten birthing going on that it was not unusual to see almost on any given day a mother cat with a kitten in her mouth going somewhere in the barn or other out buildings. I do not remember what I called "Felix" after that.

Lake Surprise and the Frog Ponds

The land that comprised the Shewman farm was made up of several different soil types. There were some that were muck lands. Muck is decayed vegetation that has taken perhaps centuries to form. Quite often, the water table is very close to the surface of the land. As expected, this land is very wet and, unless drained, is never farmable.

Other parts of the farm were hilly and very rocky. We had such a field that was in pasture most of the time. Dad might decide to do crop rotation and plant corn in this particular field, but most of the time in was in pasture. This parcel was much higher than the land around it. At the very top of the hill the land lay fairly level with a small depression about two hundred feet square and perhaps two feet deep in the lowest part. In the wintertime, snow would collect in this low part. Then when the sun came out and things warmed up, the snow would melt. This became a pretty interesting body of water to young lads like my nephews and myself.

The weather in Indiana could change quickly. Overnight the small glimmering body of water became a frozen lake of ice. My nephew, Gene, and I dubbed this fun place, Lake Surprise. We would load up our sleds with all of the camping equipment that we had. This was not much but would include such things as dry wood, dry matches, coal-oil, and perhaps a few slices of bread and a couple raw onions. We would fashion a couple of hockey sticks out of whatever material we could find. We would add a couple of homemade pucks and away we would go.

Sometimes we would spend all day pretending to skate around on the ice, hitting a makeshift puck with makeshift sticks. We would find some pieces of wood in the swamp that lay to the west of this field. We would start a small campfire on the edge of Lake Surprise and sit on our sleds beside it, drinking in the coziness. Gene and I would dream ahead to the future of hunting and fishing trips that one day we just knew we would take. We would pretend that we were the Daniel Boones or the Henry Wares of our time. We had no cares, just the present to spend on our thoughts and imaginings.

The swamp area just west of Lake Surprise contained muck soil as described earlier. A couple of men came by and convinced my dad that they knew what they were doing in wanting to clean off the swamp and plant potatoes. Dad agreed to let them do it. I am not sure whether he cleared this with Mr. Shewman, the landlord.

At any rate, they worked feverishly at their task but made the mistake of piling up the brush and setting fire to it. The brush burned down into the ground and the muck caught on fire. I remember the muck fires burning most of the summer and into early winter. People would come out from Akron and all around to see the fireworks at night. The sparks and cherry red coals made an unusual display during the dark hours of the night. The ground smoldered long enough that large holes formed. Some of the holes may have been as large as twenty feet across and as much as six feet deep.

After the winter snows and the spring rains had come, the holes filled up with water which did not go away. Any kind of body of water fascinated me, and this freak accident had given me my own small lakes. I noticed on some of my first visits to the ponds that there were frogs sitting on the banks. Soon, I discovered small fish swimming around in the ponds. I wondered just how this could be. I asked around and was told that on occasion the wind would swoop down into a lake and pick up small fish near the surface and deposit them nearby. If they landed in water they could survive. This must have been the case with my ponds. Rock Lake was close by and I just knew that was where the fish had come from. The wind must have picked up some minnows and put them in my ponds.

This stroke of good fortune fell right down the alley of my nephew, Gene and me. We were looking for the opportunity to stretch our outdoor wings. First of all, we named the area the Frog Ponds. Gene and I approached my mom with the idea of trying to catch the small fish that were in the ponds. We did not have even the first piece of fishing tackle, but Mom was creative. She took some long straight pins and made a couple of very crude fish hooks. Gene and I cut some small limbs and made a pole for each of us. We used some of Mom's sewing thread for line and off to catch the fish we went.

The fish turned out to be too small for the large hooks that Mom had fashioned from the pins. They would not bite, and we soon lost our interest in trying to catch them. We wanted to, but were not experienced enough to get the job done. We should have asked my brother, Gene's dad, to help. He had loads of tackle.

Gene and I did notice that the frog population was increasing. We would select a stick and slip quietly to the ponds edge, sometimes crawling on our stomachs. We would swing away at the frogs and sometimes land a lucky blow. It was fun to watch the frogs we missed jump into the water with a big splash. Mom cautioned us that we might destroy too many of the frogs and that we had better keep some for seed. Dean and Dale, my other nephews, joined in on this sport with us and it lasted for several summers. The muck area was ruined for farming with the large holes in the ground and it lay unused for several summers. I count this happening of nature with the help of man, (this creation of ponds of water), a rich time in my early life.

Billy, nephew Gene and Dad

The Old Hens and Their Home

One of the more important buildings on the Shewman farm was the hen house. The hen house was necessary in order to have a place to keep the laying hens corralled while they were producing eggs. Early each spring, Mom would place an order with Beshore's Feed Store in Akron for one-hundred and fifty baby chicks. The chicks could be purchased either straight run or sexed. The feed store man had ways to determine which were male and which were female. Mom usually bought pullets, the female. She did not want to feed expensive chick mash to roosters. After all, they would not produce eggs. Their only value would be in what she could get out of them when she sold them as fryers when they were about six weeks old.

Mom would put the baby chicks in the brooder house. This building was on wooden runners and could be pulled to various parts of the orchard. As the chicks grew they were allowed to run outside during the daytime within a fenced-in area. Changing the location of the building from year-to-year helped keep the possibility of diseases from being passed from flock to flock each year. The brooder house had an oil-fired brooder stove that kept the small chicks warm. One of the tasks in getting the chicks started was to keep them from crowding together and smothering one another. They didn't seem to be too bright. If one chick started to peck another and there was evidence of blood it would sometimes turn the entire flock into a cannibalistic mood. Part of the assignment in daily observation of the flock was to be on the alert for such activity and separate them.

Come fall of the year if all went reasonably well, we would end up with around one-hundred and thirty young pullets. This was about the maximum for the hen house.

The brooder house and Mom with some of her chicks.

Invariably there would be a few roosters and, as soon as they were a couple of pounds in size, they ended up on the dinner table. If there were more than we could eat at that time there was always someone stopping by selling something who would usually be willing to take the young roosters in trade. I have seen the time when we would trade a bushel of wheat or a couple of roosters for a year's subscription to some farm magazine that Dad or Mom thought had pretty pictures in it.

When Mom would start to find small pullet eggs here and there around the brooder house or in the fenced lot, she knew that it would soon be time to "pen up the pullets." Mother looked forward to this time because it meant that the older hens must be sold and this would mean cash. With this new money on the scene she could buy that certain item, be it a piece of furniture or new linoleum for one of the rough old floors that were in all of the rooms.

The young pullets soon became the hens of the henhouse. They quickly caught on to what was expected of them and would cackle and sing with much merriment as they produced egg after egg. All of this was watched closely by my mom, for the egg money was important to her as she worked and saved for the needs of her family.

It always seemed to me that Mom had the job of keeping our family's many activities well oiled. Mom wanted very much for her family to have a reasonable amount of pleasure. Her ability to stretch the few coins that made it into her lap apron was phenomenal. When I wanted to participate in some school function or just wanted a ten cent pack of small fire crackers the apron came into play. She would get the egg money jar from the kitchen cabinet and sit down in the chair by the north kitchen window. As she sat there, the apron made a natural bowl shaped pocket between her knees.

Mom wearing the apron that became the family financial desk when her family had those special financial needs.

She would pour the coins from the egg money jar into her lap and start her method of budgeting. First she had to determine that the next few day's purchases from the local bread man were covered. Sometimes another need would surface and she would put back some coins to take care of it. I generally was given sufficient funds to take care of my request. There were times when she had to say no. Mom's way of saying no never came across to me as harsh. I never made a fuss. I had the utmost confidence in her accounting ability and respected her decisions.

One of the last chores that someone had to do after supper was to shut the henhouse door. The outside door was locked each evening and then reopened the next morning. There was a screen door behind the outside door that was kept latched all the time. The outside door was opened each morning for ventilation. In cold weather both doors would remain closed. Once it became dark the hens would settle down and perch themselves on the roosts provided in the henhouse.

I would take a flashlight with me to see what I was doing when I had the "close the door" assignment. Sometimes I would shine the light around inside of the henhouse and I would see as many as three dozen rats. The rats would be standing on their hind feet eating mash out of the feeders Dad had provided for the hens. The rats infuriated my dad. He always invested in ammunition for the old twenty-two rifle we had. I was encouraged to shoot rats just as soon as Dad thought I was big enough.

I found that the best time to shoot rats was at dusk. The rats would come out from underneath the henhouse to get some fresh air. I would slip up to the corner of the henhouse and peek around it. Sure enough, I would see eight or ten rats running around a few feet from the hole they had come out of. I would take a good aim at a rat and shoot. I would have to stop and reload the single shot rifle we had. This would take a little time and the rats would scurry back down the holes to the protection of the floor of the henhouse. The interesting thing about their actions was they would only have three or four holes and sometimes there would be so many rats out at one time that they would have to line up at the holes to take turns getting back down. I might get a second shot when this was the case.

On several occasions, my brother, Adrian, left his bolt action rifle with me. With this type of weapon I could get several shots off before all of the rats would get their turn at re-entering the holes. I tried to interest my cats in the rats. They would do pretty good by them for a while, but they soon became tired of that kind of a diet.

My brother, Forrest, would park his Model A Ford so that the headlights lined up with the edge of the henhouse. He would get the car into position during the daylight hours. When it became dusk, he would position himself across a fender with his rifle. I would be inside the car ready to turn the lights on at his given signal. I found this to be big sport and was ready to participate at the drop of a hat.

More Rats and Wheeling Manure

Life on the farm created another interesting job for me. The area of the barn where the milk cows spent considerable time needed close attention. This fell my lot after brother, Irvin, left for college. The cows would arrive at the barn around five o'clock each evening. They just knew what time it was and fully expected to be allowed to enter that part of the barn we called the cow barn. They had spent the day leisurely wandering about the pasture fields of the farm. They were tired of eating grass and could remember the good tasting ground feed they had the night before.

There were times that I had to go to the pasture and drive the cows up to the barn at milking time. This might take place when they would be in a new part of the pasture. All the cows had their own particular place in the cow barn that they called home and we called stanchions. They would go to the same stanchion each evening, put their heads through and wait patiently for someone to fasten them in. It is interesting how they, too, became creatures of habit.

After the cows had dined on the ground feed they found waiting for them, we would pitch hay into the manger. Sometimes this would be alfalfa hay and at other times we would use soybean hay. All of this caused the cows to respond freely to what we might call "mother nature" and created a real mess. The cow barn had a cement floor with a built-in gutter about four inches in depth immediately below the rear of the cow. A lot of the time the cows did not cooperate on an accurate basis. They would miss the gutter. Sometime during the day I would use a scoop shovel, a wheelbarrow and an old broom to tidy up the place.

Each spring we would fork the previous winter's cow barn cleanings into a manure spreader and spread it over the fields we intended to cultivate that summer. We would start the accumulation fresh each summer and on through the winter months. I would add each wheelbarrow load to the previous deposit until by late spring there would be quite a long ridge of manure working its way from the barn door eastward, waiting to be loaded and spread. I would sweep the area with a broom and then sprinkle lime about the area I had cleaned. We would leave the unsoiled bedding and add to it as needed.

I kept the rifle close by and would often see large rats crawling over the corn in the corn crib that was part of the barn. I had to be very careful not to shoot through the roof. I managed to eliminate many of the pesky critters while cleaning the cow barn. I have read articles wherein some declare that rats have cost the farmers millions of dollars over the years. I do know that they destroyed and consumed a lot of grain on the Shewman farm.

Jelly Bread, Can Rubbers, and The Old Hens

When I was quite small Mom would allow the hens to run loose in the yard around the henhouse. The story was told about my brother, Irvin. It seems that he was eating a piece of jelly bread while walking around in the yard close to the henhouse. The story goes that some of the jelly fell off of the bread to the ground. In his haste to retrieve the jelly, he picked up some hen droppings by mistake and placed it on his bread and ate it. This was a natural mistake because hen droppings do look very much like some kinds of jelly. My older brothers teased him about this for years.

Whenever the hens were allowed to be loose they would often go under the granary building. The building rested on large boulders and had about twenty inches of clearance from the ground. This made for another good country boy sport. My nephews and I would crawl on our hands and knees or wiggle on our stomachs under the granary. Mom would discard canning jar rubbers that would no longer seal. We would follow the hens around trying to toss the rubbers around their necks.

We would see some of the evidence of our marksmanship days later as we would observe some of the hens marching around with a red can ring still around their necks. Mom did not seem to mind too much. She continued to pass on the old can rubbers from time to time. She knew we needed things to do.

Billy and Doc the dog.

5

YOUNG

IMPRESSIONS

Cold Nights and the Coal Shed

My early memories of the Shewman farm in the winter time are that it was always cold. We burned coal that was purchased a couple of tons at a time from a man named Grogg who lived in Disco, a very small town two miles south of the Shewman farm. After I was big enough, one of my duties was to take the coal bucket to the coal shed. I was to fill the bucket with coal that I had broken into pieces so they would be small enough to go through the stove door. I was to keep the bucket full all times that I was present at the house. It seemed to me that on those cold nights the bucket was forever becoming empty.

The coal shed, first called the wood shed, generated a lot of interest and created many imaginary situations in my young mind. The shed had been added to the house and did not have a foundation but rested on short posts made of stone.

The coal shed figures prominently in my memories of Christmas 1933. My brother, Irvin, somehow managed to put together three dollars and ninety-five cents and made sure that there was a nice shiny new Daisy five-hundred shot air rifle under the tree with my name on it. Mom and Dad must have helped out. The gun was there on Christmas morning.

Irvin and I tested the air rifle in the coal shed by swinging open the loading door on the east side of the shed. That particular Christmas morning was cold and a snow storm was in progress. We did not want to go out in the storm so we swung open the small door used to unload the coal and shot the gun through the open door at some selected target in the orchard. I remember telling Irvin that I wanted him to shoot the gun first just in case

there was a real bullet in the chamber. At this writing this
same "Daisy Air Rifle" is a keepsake of my oldest son.

1933 Daisy five-hundred shot air rifle

My brother, Adrian, during one of his animal interest phases, decided to raise rabbits. When you raise rabbits you never know how many you have raised. The rabbits decided that underneath the coal shed would make a nice home. Some of them would go under the coal shed to stay at night. When I was in the coal shed I would hear the rabbits scuffling about, and would imagine all sorts of scary things that might be happening to them. The shed did not have a window or any kind of provision for lighting and was very spooky. I remember quickly filling the coal bucket or other assignment I had been given and hurriedly returning to the safety of the main house.

Hot Summer Nights and Their Sounds

The upstairs bedrooms were very cold in the winter and were very hot and humid on those hot Indiana summer nights. But on those summer nights, I would sleep with the windows wide open. All of the sounds of the night seemed so close. The birds in the trees of the nearby swamp and orchard, and the insects under my window, all had their loud clamor. They seemed to be crying out for attention and to be heard by others of their species. This

118

all sounded so distant and so magical to a young lad growing up on the farm. Some of those years I would be the only one sleeping in the big upstairs. Sometimes I thought perhaps the birds and the bugs were trying to get my attention. I often stayed awake for what seemed like hours imagining all sorts of things about the sounds of the night. There wasn't a television or even a radio to see or hear weird and scary stories to put ideas in my head. My imagination must have been fueled by stories told earlier in the evening as we sat around in the dark after eating the evening meal. Even now I can hear some of those night sounds, echoing through the many years, reminding me of those nights in the upstairs of that large and mystic house on the Shewman farm.

Furniture Down the Stairs

The summer nights on the farm could also be very scary when the dark skies rolled and tossed with thunder and lightning. This part of the world is famous for the intensity of its thunderstorms, which deliver some of the noisiest and most frightening displays of fireworks imaginable.

As a little fellow, I can remember thinking as the thunder boomed, that someone surely must be pushing furniture down the stair steps. Growing up in that area, I knew that lightning does strike once in awhile. One time while I was living there it did strike, hitting a radio antenna wire that was attached to the well house. The lightning followed the wire and entered the house. Whenever storms came up someone was designated to hurry upstairs to close any open windows.

On this particular evening my brother, Adrian, was dispatched to close the windows. As he came into the room where the antenna wire entered the house, he was startled by a ball of fire that the lightning had produced when it struck the house. The room was filled instantly with dust and the smell of burnt plaster and lathe. Large chucks of plaster fell all around, but my brother was not hit. He scurried to another room just in time to see the ball of fire go through one open window and out through another.

This incident added much gusto to the stories we had to tell around the post suppertime story hour. For days, I could smell the aroma of hot plaster dust. All of this excitement did not do much for my ability to fall asleep very fast from then on. As a youngster, I did not have any way to measure my security or if I indeed had anything to be afraid of. When the thunder boomed and the lightning flashed, I listened and watched in awe.

I remember very clearly, as a little fellow of about four, sitting in a little rocking chair in the front yard under the two pear trees that were beside State Road #114. Dad was a very good farmer and certainly had a green thumb. He could grow watermelons with the best and had quite a reputation in the community for his melons. Dad kept a close watch on the progress of the melons and of their ripening.

When Dad thought the melons were ready he would take the back seat out of the 1926 Model T Ford and drive it to the patch edge. Dad would select the ripe melons and fill up the back seat then drive the car to the front of the house. He would place the melons on the ground under one of the pear trees and then instruct me on how to price them and how to sell them.

This must have been my first business experience. I could even plug a melon to prove to the potential buyer that it was ripe. I knew how to tell by thumping which melons were the ripest and made sure that I would only plug those. I did not want to waste a melon by putting a hole in it. I got pretty good at this and I do not remember having to throw out any melons. If we had a green melon

121

show up, we would split it open and put it by the chicken house for the hens to peck out. They would clean the melon out right up to the very last possible peck. I knew the prices and would quote them to the buyers. After they were satisfied with a purchase they would give me a piece of money. I would run into the house and show the money to my mother. I would tell her the type of melon and the price Dad had put on it. My mom would make the correct change and I would run the change back out to the waiting customer. All of this happened before I started going to school.

Dealing in money just seemed to fall naturally to me. I did not have the slightest thought, at that time, that I would spend all of my adult years dealing in monies all about the world, or that I would be so heavily involved in business and financial administration.

Dad, Bent Masks and I Can Too

My dad used to tell me stories of his baseball endeavors. He told me that when he lived in Salt Lick, Kentucky, he was the pitcher on a local independent baseball team. He told me that he threw the ball so hard that it dented catchers' masks. Dad said that the team had a difficult time locating anyone that would stand behind the plate and catch for him. As Dad continued to pitch against local teams of that area, his reputation began to grow and so did the team's. Batters would be so afraid of my dad's fast pitch that they would just stand near the plate and only poke at the ball.

A team from Louisville heard about Dad's team and wanted to play them. Louisville was good enough in those days that they could have been a minor league or farm team. According to Dad, Louisville beat them pretty bad and his team's reputation dwindled. All of this probably encouraged me to say that I was a baseball pitcher when the boys at school went out to play at recess and at the noon hour. I remember that I dearly loved the game and played it at every opportunity. We had areas around the school building that were large enough for little grade schoolers like us to use.

Here Comes the Milkman!

One of the options that my dad had in his arrangement with the landlord, was to be able to keep milk cows. This meant that if we milked cows and wanted to sell the milk, we had to have a way of transporting the milk each day to the dairy in Akron. Dad contracted with a local milk hauler to stop by each morning after the milking was done. He drove a large covered truck that kept the milk shaded on the hot summer mornings. He would come by to get the milk very early in the morning and was able to get the milk into the Akron dairy before the sun became too high in the sky. This required all of the farmers on the route to get up very early. They had to get their milking completed and cooled and standing by in eight gallon cans for pick-up. All of the farmers kept the milk cans in water tanks in milk houses that were shaded from the hot summer sun.

Milk was weighed at the dairy and each milk hauler was paid by the farmer for each hundred pounds of milk he delivered to the dairy. The dairy would take the hauling fee from the farmer's check and pay the hauler. Paul Strong was the first driver that I can remember.

When I was very little, even before I was old enough to go to school, I would play out in the yard, sometimes out behind the hen house. I was very carefully instructed to be in the house when the milk driver came. This meant that no matter how far I was away from the kitchen door and all of the security that it offered, I had to run like mad to make this possible. When I would hear the milk truck driver slow up and shift gears at the bottom of the slight hill behind the house, I would drop whatever I was doing and tear to the house. Naturally the older I became the farther out into the orchard I would go to play.

The path that was the shortest route to the house crossed over the lane that the milk truck driver used in his approach to the milk house. I wonder what went through Paul Strong's mind when he saw this flash of a small farm lad zip past the front of his truck. My sister, Christeen, said that I would run into the house and hide behind the kitchen stove. I remember playing a lot behind the kitchen stove. It was cozy and warm in the winter time.

At some point in those early years it occurred to me that I should not run any more but instead just hide. I would hide behind the hen house or cob shed or perhaps the meat house, so that Paul Strong could not see me. Then I was safe. Paul Strong must have had many a chuckle as he picked up the Shrout's milk. He probably made a game of it, trying to guess just what my moves would be after he shifted truck gears.

Dad, Pood and Paperhanging

We very seldom painted any of the interior walls of the house on the Shewman place. Wall papering seemed to be the thing to do in those days. Dad would get out the step ladders, the walking planks, the brushes and lots of flour and water for paste. I do not recall seeing much plain or mild designed wall paper. The design was wild and potent, with loud colors and lots of huge flowers all over it.

Dad could usually do a reasonable job on the side walls, but when it came to the ceilings he always had trouble. Even knowing that there would be a problem, Dad kept trying anyway. As he proceeded down the walking plank, most of the time the paper would fall behind him as he brushed it out in front of him. I thought that this sort thing was kind of funny and on occasion chuckled out loud. Dad did not think it very funny and most of the time would in his anger wad up the fallen paper in a ball and throw it as far as he could. You could count on the next step to be Dad calling up our neighbor, Pood, to come finish the job.

Pood was a nickname for a man who lived in our neighborhood who spoke with a deep guttural sound.

He really did do a lot of grunting as he walked back and forth on the walk board. As Pood smoothed the ceiling wall paper, it flowed on and on so endlessly. I used to watch in amazement as Pood made something that had spoofed my dad seem simple. I had thought my dad could do anything.

Pood would roll a cigarette from a sack of Bull Duram tobacco, light it, and let in dangle from the corner of his mouth. Pood would walk back and forth on the walk board, smoking the cigarette he had hand-rolled. I would hear Pood cussing in that low growling voice. It seemed to me that the more he cussed and growled the better the paper went on. Sometimes when Pood was not available to do it, Vinee, the neighbor from across the huckleberry swamp, could be hired to do the job.

Go Ahead and Wreck It

Most little boys watch their fathers and older brothers drive the family car and wish that they could also have this wonderful, fun privilege of driving. I watched my dad drive the 1926 Model T Ford and observed all of the procedures that he went through. I just knew that I could drive the car. I practiced in the car when it was unoccupied and felt that I had everything down pretty good. I waited for the right opportunity to make this very special request of Dad. The time had to be just right. Dad could be short in some of his responses to other things I had wanted to do. I must be careful this time, I thought.

Then one day, Dad and Mom and I had been out in the country east of the house. About a mile from the Shewman farm I posed the request of the century with some fear and trembling. "Dad, I know how to drive the car, can I drive it the rest of the way back to the house?" "You can't do it," Dad said. I persisted and he made a remark that I shall never forget. "Oh, go on and wreck it."

Well, this little seven year old got into the driver's seat. I swelled myself up to look the biggest possible and started the vehicle down the road. The Model T had three pedals: a brake, a reverse and a clutch. There was a hand clutch that sort of worked as a hand brake. We had it tied back with a rope and had to let it loose at the right time. These procedures I did quite well and pulled the car up to the bottom of the hill driveway leading up into our yard. I knew I might be stretching my abilities if I tried to take the car up the small incline of the hill. Mom was amazed at what her little guy could do. So was Dad.

All Those Doors

When I think back to the room arrangements in the Shewman farm house, the most outstanding thing that comes to my mind are all of the doors. The middle room of the lower level, the dining room, had seven doors and two windows. The kitchen had two windows and four doors. The front room had three doors and two windows. This adds up to a lot of windows and doors.

I do not think that any of the doors or windows had a secure lock on them. No one seemed to be concerned about locking the doors. Most people left their homes unlocked. We had one door that was of some concern to my mother. The door leading from the kitchen to the washroom had a small sliding latch in the door. Mom would always make sure the the latch was in locked position before going to bed. I do not recall any other door causing a special worry to her. Many of the other doors were poorly fastened, if at all. I can still hear my mom calling to those of us still in the kitchen area at bedtime to make sure the kitchen door was latched.

Many times since and even in recent years, I have awakened from a dream in which someone was trying to get in through one of the many doors. They found one that was unlocked or so minimally secured that they just pushed it in. No time while living at the farm do I recall anyone breaking in, but the many doors of the house, have made a vivid impression in my memory bank.

The Dinner Table and Afterwards

I have warm memories of our family sitting around the large dinner table on the Shewman farm. We always ate in the kitchen around a huge table that could seat the seven of us at the same time. We had a round table that had several leaves in the dining room but that was seldom used.

All of our meals were taken in the kitchen. I am sure this was the practical thing to do. The food was cooked in the kitchen so it was nice and handy to take it off of the South Bend brand cook stove that Mom used to exercise all of her interesting and tasty talents. The stove had two warming closets in the rear of the superstructure which made an excellent place to store leftovers which did not need refrigeration.

When we came home from school we would all make a mad dash to see what was in the closets left over from the noon meal. I think Mom planned ahead for this event and prepared just a little extra for the two of them so she could be ready for her famished children when they came in from school. When I was in the early grades, I could never get there in time. My older brothers fought for and cleaned out everything that Mom had left there.

There came a day when I could participate and recall doing so. I would grab a piece of corn bread, and, of course, I knew where to find an onion. A quick change from school clothes to our farm attire and away we would go to the barn to start the evening chores. These extra morsels of food would have to last us until we made it back to the house after the milking was done.

Table manners were very scarce at meal time. My brother, Adrian, would sit down to the kitchen table before any of the rest of us. This did not meet with my mom's approval. There were times that he would stick his fork into what appeared to be the largest piece of meat on the platter to establish his right of possession. Mother would scold him, but it never seemed to make any difference.

Mother would sit at one end of the table and my dad at the other end. Adrian was on the corner next to Mom

131

with Irvin next to him. I would sit at the end of the table by Dad, just around the corner from Irvin. To Dad's left would be brother Emerson and next to him my sister, Christeen. Although the food was simple there always seemed to be plenty of it. Dad was not into idle chatter, or we probably would have had more times of laughter during the meal. To me this was a very special time and I remember it with much pleasure.

Mother was a good cook and could really do a superb job with anything she attempted to bake. Mom would serve my dad coffee straight from the cook stove and I would see the coffee bubble up and down in his cup. He could really drink it hot. Sometimes he would saucer it, but most of the time he could take it right off the stove. One thing that stands out in my memory is my dad waiting until the coffee was about to run over and then telling my mom, "thats enough." I wonder what would have happened if he had not told her to stop.

These were the days before television came on the scene and made captives of us. I remember the times we did not have a radio that was working. We did not have electricity and our radio was powered by batteries. A set of "B" batteries was needed and they cost a lot more than we had to spend on such things during most of those years of my growing up.

Very little news was current by the time we heard it. Storms would come through Northern Indiana and really tear up things. We would not hear about it until days afterwards. The town of Akron had a newspaper, but we seldom subscribed to it. It would generally report cars running into the ditch or someone's barn catching fire. Some neighbor would have an active radio and would get the word out eventually on what was happening in the world around us.

The party line function of our wall telephone was one means of communication. More than one neighbor would listen in, or "eaves drop" as we called it. It was the thing to do and was not considered inappropriate.

Life went on and each family found its own particular method of spending the leisure time of the evenings and weekends. On the Shewman farm, we had a room next to the kitchen that we called the "washroom." We stored the washing machine in this room and Mom did the clothes washing there in good weather. On the really cold days she would pull the machine into the kitchen and wash there.

The washroom was also the location of the drinking water bucket. We all drank out of the same cup that sat by the bucket. One day my brother Irvin was with Dad and Mom at a neighbor's house where the lady of the house did not look too tidy or clean. The story goes that Irvin wanted a drink, so used his left hand to hold the dipper, thinking that this side of the cup probably did not have much use. To his surprise, he heard the lady of the house comment, "Oh, you are are left-handed, too." I do not know how we kept from passing colds about with all of us using the same cup. No one ever made much of it.

The wash room area made an excellent room to gather in after supper. We would sit on the floor in front of the south screened-in door and leave the north door open for a cross breeze. We would do this almost every evening in the summertime. We might start by sitting outside, but the mosquitoes would quickly run us inside. This time in our lives allowed Dad and Mom the opportunity to pass on to us the basic principals of life.

During some of those evenings of pleasant conversation, Dad would inform us of our important heritage and the family roots. Even though we came from very modest beginnings, I never felt that I was shorted in my allowance of family ancestral assets. I was made to understand and feel proud of who I was and from whence I came. I did not have today's attitude of wanting everything that came down the pike. I found great pleasure in the little things. Consequently, I developed skills in making things and was content to make things do.   Dad's tales of his childhood were fascinating to me.   I could listen for hours without tiring.   Bedtime quickly came, and I would go with my imagination working in high gear.

In the wintertime, we would move to the room with the big Ray Boy heating stove and listen to the wind blowing through the cracks around the loose-fitting windows. We would watch the snow build up into huge drifts.   Those of us in school would be hoping for a "no school day" as the snow continued into the night.   Dad would still find time to spin his tales and, in his way, encourage us to be good citizens. It was important to him that we gain adulthood with a generous portion of good common sense.   This always seemed to be the familiar thread that Dad would weave in and out through his stories.

Even though I didn't know at that time what was around the corner in the big city of life, I felt confident that I could cope with anything that came my way.   Dad instilled a certain assurance of self-reliance that made its mark on me.

Charley and Pete
and Old Horses Cry

Horses could be found on most working farms during the 'Thirties. The number of horses to be found on a farm depended on the acreage under cultivation and if there was a tractor present. While Dad was farming the Shewman farm, he tried to keep three healthy horses at a time. Sometimes this meant having four on the farm at the same time but very seldom did Dad put a team of four together. Some more affluent neighbors had as many as six horses. Most farming assignments required a team of three for the heavier work. I recall some farmers using a team of four when pulling a heavy wheat binder when the weather was very hot. A lot of tasks could also be performed by a two-horse team.

While living on the farm we had one horse that was always there and could always be counted on to more than do his share. This horse's name was Charley. On some cold snowy evenings, cars that became stranded in snow drifts close by would come to the house and ask Dad and Charley to pull them out of the drift.

For most of my time on the farm Charley's team partner was a horse named Pete. Charley and Pete were something else when it came to pulling a heavy load. They could pull some very heavy loads in proportion to their size. A team must learn how to work together. One horse cannot lurch ahead of the other. The double tree that they are attached to must stay even in order to have the most efficiency. I have seen horse teams that kept the double tree sawing back and forth and they got nowhere.

Dad driving Charley and Pete, pulling a wagon box mounted on snow skis. Pete has the white blaze on his nose. Charley always worked on the left side of the team.

Dad would harness the horses one at a time in the barn while each was in its stall. He would bring them out one by one and lead them through the smaller wooden gate by the the granary. Each horse would stand where Dad would leave him while he went back for another. He had them trained well. Driving lines had to be attached and then away he would go to hook them to whatever he was going to use that day. If he were breaking ground in the field, he would have left the plow in the field.

When I was about twelve, I started harnessing the horses. It was difficult at first. Harness was heavy and in having to shape it to fit the horse's back as you placed it on them was quite a chore for a young fellow. But I caught on and soon found I could I do it as well as Dad.

Along with harnessing, my dad required a lot of care be given his horses. They had to be curried and brushed. He believed in taking good care of his animals. Without the horses there would be no farming. Dad made sure that they had corn and oats each noon when they returned to the barn from the field. We had to watch Charley very carefully because he knew how to open the entrance door to the horse stalls. He would go in and eat the other horse's rations before they could get in. I remember that some of the time my duties were to get the corn and oats in the grain box part of the manger before Dad would arrive.

While all of this noontime horse feeding activity went on, Mother would be getting the food on the table for Dad. There was a time that we had a large dinner bell mounted on a post that Mom could ring to notify those in the field that it was dinner time. Most of the time Dad did not have a pocket watch but knew when to stop for dinner.

The third horse of our three horse team had several names. We always had Charley and Pete, but their third team partner seemed to change every few years. One horse was named Dick and he needed lots of room to get up and down. Dad had to make his stall larger than the others. Then we had Dan, whose feet always hurt him. They were so big and were always breaking off at the edge of the hoof. I saw Dad on many occasions take out his case pocket knife and trim old Dan's feet.

Dad used a three horse team to pull the fourteen-inch single bottom riding breaking plow. He would plow one round and then rest the team a few minutes. He would repeat the process over and over, and as the field became smaller he would adjust the rest stops to the shortening of the rounds. The hard rocky ground, coupled with the many hills to go up and down, made the plowing task a real chore. Muck ground was much softer and much easier and therefore faster. Not all muck ground was tillable. Sometimes the water table was very close to the surface. A

team of horses is very heavy, and it was very easy for one
of them to push his leg through a soft spot where water
was close to the surface. There was a time or two that
Dad did get a horse down in the soft ground, and it was a
little scary. He always was afraid to use Dick in the muck
since he had such a difficult time in getting to his feet.
Dad always rescued them.

Ol' Pete became almost totally blind. He must have
contracted some kind of horse eye disease. He would run
into the fences and walk sideways down the corn row
trying to see out of the side of his blinders. The bridles on
horses had eye shades, or blinders, to keep them from
looking back to see what was hooked to them.

One day Dad was using Pete to pull a one horse
single row cultivator and Ol' Pete was tramping the corn
down something terrible. Dad became more and more
irritated. It seems that I was supposed to be down in
the field helping him and I failed to show. Dad left
Ol' Pete in the field and came to the house to get me. He
found me reading a funny paper. I remember well Dad
catching me by the back of my neck with his very large
hand and half dragging me to the corn field. He wanted
me to sit up on Pete and steer him up and down the rows
to keep him from tramping on the corn. Up onto Ol' Pete
he threw me and there is where I remained the rest of the

working part of the day. I knew that when Dad said he wanted something I had better do it.

Sometime shortly after this happening, Dad felt that it was time to get rid of Pete. As the truck pulled out of the barn yard with Ol' Pete on board, Charley reached his head as far as he could over the barnyard fence. It looked to me that he wanted to see his old buddy for as long as he could. As Ol' Pete disappeared from view around the barn, he could be heard in a very pitiful nickering sound. Charley returned the farewell neigh and I thought I saw tears in his eyes. This was so sad to a young farm boy.

Charley continued for several years to be the same old reliable horse he always was. His new team partner was a young mare we named Tops. Dad purchased Tops from a farmer who lived south of Gilead. Charley and Tops became our main team and worked very well together. Dad contracted the services of a stud horse through a local horse breeder and Tops became a mother. I was very excited at the news of our new colt. Dad named the new colt Prince.

Charley was a gentle horse and there were many times that I would ride him either bareback or with an old English saddle that showed up at the farm. The daily relationship that a farmer had with his horses caused a natural fondness for one another. I just knew that Charley and my dad were good buddies. After all, they spent many hours together over the years of farming the Shewman farm.

6

BILLY'S ENTERPRISES

Letting Our Light Shine

Early in my life I became aware of the need for orderliness. For some reason or another, I always wanted to see things in a neat order around the house. I remember the old coal-oil lamps and the dirty, smudgy glass globes that always looked untidy each evening before lighting. As soon as Mom would allow me to do so, I started polishing the lamp globes when I came in from school.

I recall going about the living room and straightening up this and that. I remember never liking the way I would find the top of the dining room table. Whatever mail had come to our house during the day and anything Dad or Mom had pulled out to read would still be on the table just where they had tossed it. After shining up the lamp globes, I would fill them with coal-oil from the old five gallon can Dad had purchased in Akron.

Cement Baseballs

I discovered a new use for the old discarded balls of dirty wall paper cleaner. At some point in time, I picked up one that had dried out and was very hard. I bounced it on the cement. The ball of cleaner reacted like a real baseball and bounced back at me, at least a little. These were hard times and I had no money to buy baseballs. I remember thinking, "Wow, maybe I have struck on something. Maybe this could be used for baseballs."

After the next wall paper cleaning, I saved the discarded dirty cleaner. I watched carefully and made sure that before they became hard I shaped them to as perfectly round a baseball as I could. I placed the balls on top of the well house roof and let the sun do its work. I used the finished product on more than one occasion when I needed a baseball and also when I needed a new challenge. Did those balls ever sting your hands when you hit them with a bat! They also stung pretty hard when you attempted to catch them. I could just imagine what the poor old setting hens thought as they waited patiently for their eggs to hatch and the rock-like balls came slamming into the cob shed. We knocked off about all of the paint that was on the side of the building by using such hard objects for balls.

Battle Axe

Another game that Gene and I invented we called "battle axe." Dad fed corn on the cob to the horses. He would put the corn in the manger trough. When the horses had eaten the corn off of the cob, Dad would toss the cobs out onto the barn floor in front of the manger. My nephew, Gene, and I started throwing the cobs at each other. I'm sure this sport must have started by accident. One of us, thinking it a smart thing to do, probably nailed the other on the side of his head with a cob. Several of the neighborhood boys would come over on Sunday afternoons. We would choose up sides and the battle would begin. The one who was able to get the freshly emptied cobs would be at an advantage. The horses would leave a heavy salivation that made the cobs very heavy. We played this game for hours, usually until someone got a hit that hurt too much to continue the game.

The Granary--Broadway On the Farm

One of my favorite buildings on the Shewman farm was the granary building. Along with the storing of wheat and oats, Dad would use the front part of the granary for a workshop. He would keep his hand tools and other surplus mending supplies in the building. Whenever the back half of the building was not too full, I would move what few pieces happened to be there to the front part. I would then use the cleared area of about twenty by ten feet for new play projects.

Sometimes this area became a small basketball court. Other times I would use the area to stage some of

146

my play productions; I had started to write plays. This was the beginning of "Billy, the playwright." I assigned parts to my nephews and made tickets to sell for the plays. I would make tickets by the hundreds. I must have thought that I was going to attract all of Fulton County to what I just knew would be a smash hit. The largest audience I recall was two. My sister, Christeen, and my niece, Namona, gave two cents each and were brave enough to witness our endeavors. My mom came a time or two. She wanted to register her approval of our theatrical attempts.

The granary also housed some of my early engineering feats. Mom allowed me to take the wind-up motor from the RCA Victrola. I mounted the motor on a platform in the middle of the front room of the granary. I nailed empty thread spools all over the rafters and doorways. To these spools I attached string belts that allowed them to turn each other as they rambled all over the building. I found it fascinating to watch as many as fifty spools all turning at the same time. I knew Dad was as fascinated because he did not insist that I remove them right away. He liked to watch them turn. One of the reasons that I became so inspired to be creative was that there was nothing to do. No distractions, no younger brothers or sisters to entertain, just yours truly and what I could do to keep occupied.

School Bus Chicks

I became interested in an old school bus body that I saw over in neighbor Frank's barn yard. It was of the wooden type and needed a roof real bad. Frank appeared not to be using the bus for anything. I started to make plans of how this bus body could become my brooder house and that perhaps I could become rich by raising chicks. I talked to Dad about it. He said he could put a new roof on it. We made Frank an offer of five dollars and he went for it.

Dad and I went down into the swamp and cut two poles long enough to fit under the bus then fashioned a skid out of the poles. Now was the time for Charley and Pete to do their stuff. Again they came to the rescue. In my mind, I can see Dad sitting up on top of the bus body driving the team up the long lane of Frank's to our house. I was eager and proud of the opportunity to venture into my first real business effort.

Dad and I used some tar paper and roll roofing to put a new roof on the bus. For the rest of the winter I used the bus as a meeting house for one of my many clubs. I purchased a used kerosene heater at an auction sale and used it for heat. With all of the windows in the bus I received a lot of help from the sun in keeping the bus warm during the daytime.

When spring came, Mom ordered baby chicks. I also ordered fifty Buff Orfington chicks. They were of the heavy variety and were light in color. I went out one morning to check on the chicks. I found that the heater had malfunctioned and the bus was full of smoke. I opened the windows quickly and just knew that my chicks were goners. I was pleasantly surprised to see the chicks recover. For days, I could see the soot on their feathers and this acted as a constant reminder to check the heater to make sure it was cleaned and functioning properly.

Prior to this new business adventure, I had for several summers raised a few chicks using a setting hen as the caretaker. An old hen that was bent on "going set" was easily convinced to take over an instant brood of chicks. At night I would pen them up in a little chicken house about the size of a small dog house. In the daytime I would turn them loose and the old hen would take care of them, moving about the orchard scratching here and there for bugs. I would throw some cracked corn to them each day to help keep them going.

Now that I had the larger quarters in the bus, I was in a much better position to have more eggs to sell during the winter. I got to use Mom's brooder house for my hen house. Her pullets were moved into the hen house to replace the older hens she had sold. I had lots of eggs to sell. When the huckster man came by each week, I would trade my eggs for huge three-for-a-dime candy bars. I was not instructed to go easy on candy and I ate lots of it. I even received some cash, for I could not possibly spend all of the egg money on candy. The eggs provided a source for show or movie money. I was able to go to the movies at the Madrid Theater in Akron.

Sandpile Roads and Mud Pies

Immediately behind the hen house was an area of open sandy soil that the old hens enjoyed scratching and wallowing about in. On nice sunny days they would move the sand particles in and about their feathers. It helped chase the lice away. The more they scratched and stirred up the soil, the softer the ground became.

After I was big enough to be allowed to play by myself behind the hen house, I would spend hours in this soft, pleasurable sand. The area became my sandpile.

150

It was from this part of the yard that I would race to the house for security whenever the milk truck came to pick up milk. I played in this sandpile from the time I could walk.

Here I could let my mind wander and dream. I could carry out all of the imaginative ideas that came to my small but active mind. My earliest endeavors were in constructing roads. My first make-believe cars were garden hoes. I would grade out roads two hoe widths wide throughout the sandpile. When my nephews visited me, we would drag the hoes up and down the make believe roads for what seemed like hours.

As I grew older, I became even more creative. I used larger tools for vehicles, such as wheelbarrows, garden plows, onion barkers and onion cultivators. All of these tools were available since Dad would use them either in the garden or in the onion fields. Anything that had a wheel caught my imagination and I quickly thought of them as real cars.

The largest vehicle that I used was a homemade cart that Dad made out of a couple of wide rimmed wheels he found. The cart was about thirty inches wide. Now I really needed to make some much larger roads. This I did, and it now took more of my time. I would cut berms on the roads, slanting the sides of them to make small drainage ditches just like I saw the highway men do on the real roads. I would dig make believe streams or ditches across the roads and fashion bridges out of any wood scraps that I could get my hands on. I thought that it was impressive and I think my dad did also, whenever he walked through the area.

Early in life I became fascinated by store keeping. I loved to think that perhaps one day I could clerk in a store. To bridge this gap in time I entered into yet another imaginative venture. It started from the simple mud pies that most children make at some point in time. Only in my case I kept improving the method of manufacture. I got creative in using wood chips and pebbles for raisins and chocolate chips. The top of a log or a series of several boards stacked in neat rows became drying ovens and allowed me to make large quantities at one time.

Over the several months of each summer, I must have made hundreds and quite possibly thousands of mud pies. I would sell the finished products to my nephews. The means of exchange were lilac leaves and small stones. There was a reason for using the lilac leaf. There was only one lilac bush on the Shewman farm and this allowed me to control how many leaves could be in circulation at any one given time. The bush was mature enough to guarantee a bountiful source of one dollar bills throughout the summer. Small pebbles were used for change. The size denoted the worth of each stone. This pretend enterprise lasted through several summers. I never tired of that type of activity. I just outgrew it.

Rip Van Weasel

When I was at school I would hear some of my classmates tell about their trapping experiences in the drainage ditches on their farms. Muskrats were very common in our area. A good muskrat pelt would bring one to two dollars on the market. I did not have a ditch on the Shewman farm to trap. All of the ditches close by on the neighbors' places were leased to another neighbor, Ike. Ike relied on the trapping season as a cash product to get his family through the winter. I sure didn't want to bother Ike's area. I had heard stories about Ike and his traps. In fact, I heard Ike say one time, "You can mess with my wife, but don't mess my damn traps." That was enough for me not to want to bother his trapping territory.

The only possibilities for me were to trap the swamps and wooded areas on the farm. I set several traps and waited a couple of days to go look. Bright and early I set out to see what might be in my traps. I envisioned everything possible that would bring me lots of money.

One of the first critters that I caught turned out to be a weasel. I really did not know what to do first. So I beat it with a club until I was sure that there was no more life in it. I took it to the house and asked Dad what he thought it might be and if it would be worth anything to the fur collector. Dad told me that it was a weasel and it would be worth something. I hung it in a gunny sack on a nail in the inside granary wall. The weather was cold and I thought it surely would keep and not spoil. The guys at school said that they skinned their catches as they walked from one trap to another. I thought this sounded pretty swift, but I knew next to nothing about how to skin an animal.

I called the fur collector and asked him to stop by the next time he was out my way on his pickup route. In about two weeks the fur man showed up. I shook the weasel out onto the ground fully expecting it to just lie there. To my amazement it started scampering away. It was not dead after hanging in the gunny sack for the last two weeks. We caught it easily because of it's weakened condition. The fur man skinned it and gave me sixty-five cents. This seemed like a lot of cash to me!

I caught a few opossum after that, but they did not have much value. I usually got a quarter apiece for them. One time a screech owl got in my trap and I really had a time getting it out. It clawed and fought me something terrible. I did not stay in the trapping business very long after that.

My sister, Christeen, standing in front of the lilac bush that became Little Billy's "Fort Knox" when peddling his mud pies.

7

FUN THINGS

The Bike, Binder Twine
and a Stiff Neck

My older brother, Forrest, and his wife, Faun, lived and sharecropped the same as Dad, on a farm about two miles east of the Shewman farm. He attempted to be a farmer just like our dad, but Forrest never really wanted to apply himself fully to the assignment. He never did get the hang of it. I remember Dad telling us, about one day he went over to Forrest's farm looking for his son. There was a lake that joined this rented farm named Flat Lake. Dad finally located him. The team of horses was tied to the

157

fence next to the lake and my brother was out on the lake in a boat fishing.

While living at this farm, Forrest found an old castoff bicycle. It must have been in someone's junk pile or maybe he found it along the road. One day Forrest came walking the two miles or so from his farm to ours, pushing this old broken down bike. The bike could not function as a regular bike. Nothing worked, except the wheels did go around, the handlebars were there and it was steerable. Forrest said that I could have the bike. I thought that I had found a gold mine. The tires were flat and partially rotted. I managed to keep them on the rims by wrapping binder twine around them. We always had a ball of binder twine on the farm.

I would spend hours walking beside the bike pretending I was riding it. I got in the habit of leaning over the seat and sighting down across the handlebars. I did this so much that I developed a stiff neck. Dad and Mom loaded me up in the Model T and took me into Akron to see Dr. Ferry. The good Doctor took one look at me, gave me a peppermint stick and told my parents to take me home and that "little Billy" would be just fine. It goes with out saying that my dad did not like spending the one dollar that Dr. Ferry charged for our office visit when there was nothing really wrong with me.

One day I became brave enough to take the old bike to the top of the hill in front of the barn. I jumped on the bike and rode it down the hill. I really let it coast, since the propelling parts of the bike were gone or non-operable. I had no way of stopping, so I just let the bike run its course. There was not much traffic on the road in front of the barn in those days, so I was not really in much danger from cars. On the other hand, the old bike could have malfunctioned and I could have been in big trouble.

This experience was the beginning of my bike riding. My brother, Irvin, observed all of these proceedings and in some way found parts and the funds to purchase them and put together a 28-inch, high pressure tire bike for me. This was my first real workable bike. I had to stand on a box to mount.

From an Oil Can
to Real hoops

When it came to basketball, I became an avid fan. Anyone can tell you that if you live in Indiana, you are bound to want to play basketball. Young boys eat and sleep the game. "Hoosier Madness" is what they call this disease that creeps up on young lads in Indiana. I wanted to learn the game so much that I would shoot anything that half-way resembled a basketball at anything that would pass for a hoop.

Depression days meant no cash money to a sharecropper farmer. Dad did not even volunteer to talk about basketball with me. This did not deter me in the slightest. The boys at the grade school gave me the basic rules and instructions and we spent many a cold winter's day tossing someone's old leather ball at the one and only sagging hoop on the grade school playground.

My older brothers had already passed through this stage of "Hoosier Madness" and had put an old barrel stay on the side of the granary building. When I became addicted to the game I could only find an old Shell oil can to toss at the barrel stay. I would stand by the hour and shoot the oil can into the pretend hoop. The can became so battered that it was hardly recognizable. I would put on gloves and bundle up in warm clothes and brave the cold Indiana wind and snow in order to toss the can through the barrel stay.

I graduated from the oil can to an old much-used softball. The softball had come apart and lost most of its filling. I stuffed the softball with rags, then borrowed thread and a needle from Mom and sewed it up. I was really living now. This was a real ball or at least it had been one once. Not counting the fact that the old softball was much under size, it also did not bounce, and therefore I could not dribble it like the real ball at school. I yearned for any kind of rubber ball. I would dream of having my own real basketball.

I recall cutting an empty Quaker oats round box in the middle and tacking it to the wall in the wash room of the old Shewman house. This was a real test of my skill to be able to hit this small target. By this time I had scrounged up a dime and had purchased a small rubber ball at Arter's Five and Dime. I recall many good times taking on the challenge of hitting the smaller target of the oats cereal box. It was several years before I was able to purchase a real leather basketball.

The long time it took to get a real basketball did not slow my enthusiasm for the sport. If anything, I became more avid than ever and craved to be playing it at any opportunity. By the time I was a freshman in high school I was hooked. Along about this time I had started to do some work away from the farm and managed to get my first real ball. I talked Dad into helping me make a backboard. We needed some kind of hinges to mount the backboard on the inside of the barn over the door coming into the main barn floor. I had seen other barns where some of my friends had done this. Whenever we used the barn door opening to pull in a wagon load of hay, or for whatever reason, we simply pulled the backboard up out of the way. We had zero money for hinges. My dad in his usual "make do" mode of thinking, came up with the idea of cutting some leather straps from an old horse harness. They worked just fine. Now I had a much warmer place to play ball. Most of our basketball playing was in the winter time and there was no need to move the backboard up and down.

Sunday afternoons were the fun times. After dinner was over those interested would migrate to the barn and the games would begin. My brother-in-law, Bill, liked to play. He had played ball on the Silver Lake high school ball team, a community only a few miles distant. My good friend, Lester, lived a few miles south and west of us.

162

He would ride his bike over to the Shewman farm, arriving shortly after our dinner was finished. Les and I would challenge Bill to a game. Bill was older and could play somewhat rougher than we, so it seemed like a fair match.

As you approached the basket, the horse mangers were on the left side. A manger is located immediately above the grain trough. It protrudes out about a foot. The edge of the manager was very rough and had sharp splintery edges. At every opportunity we would push and shove my brother-in-law into the manager. We were mean and rough too. There were many Sunday afternoons that we gathered in the barn for a "have at it".

On many occasions, I would go to a neighbor's farm on Sunday afternoons and join in where others were congregating to enjoy the sport. The Holloway farm was close to Rock Lake. We played outside there and would only go there on a clear day. The Groningers, who lived in the Disco area, had the best barn floor for dribbling a ball. They moved the hay back and forth over boards until they became almost as smooth as a gym floor. Whit Gast was a well known local farmer who had an excellent building to play in. Whit grew potatoes and onions and had a large storage building to keep them in. In an open area in the middle of this building Whit had hung a goal for us to play basketball. On the coldest of winter days with all of the

163

produce stored around the play area, the temperature was great for shooting hoops. I was introduced to this playing area by some of Whit's day workers who were my classmates. Whit also had the only tulip garden in the Akron area. Mother's Day was a great time to purchase tulips for our mom. Whit was one of the more progressive farmers in the area. He paid a lot of attention to the agriculture department at Purdue University. This era of time was the beginning of farmers learning about commercial fertilizers and proper crop rotating.

Barn basketball, Indiana style, with nephew, Gene

Picture Shows

Akron was a small farming community town. We considered ourselves blessed by the presence of a movie theater, The Madrid. At Christmas time the Madrid owner would give the grade school students a treat and show us a movie for free. I remember the very first movie I saw. It was about grasshoppers that were lazy and did not save during the summer for the winter's use. The other side of this movie lesson were the ants. They stored up for winter. As the story went along the grasshoppers crawled through the deep snow to the ants' home and begged for something to eat. This so-called lesson has held true all through my life. I have seen many humans do the same as the grasshoppers.

We would line up outside of the school building and march down the sidewalks to the theater, which was located about six blocks in the down town area. No place is far in Akron. We went down in the afternoon and the school bus picked us up at the theater to take us home. My dad and mom did not go to picture shows. I do not think they totally disapproved but felt that this expenditure was not necessary, particularly in the time of the Depression. While I was in grade school I never went to the show except for those offered free through the school.

The Cob Shed--
Truly a Phenomenal Building

The cob shed building was about ten by twelve feet in size and was located between the house and the three-holer. During the first years of living at the Shewman farm, Dad would hitch Charley and Pete to the wagon with the side boards and go to town. The management of Halderman and Baum Grain Elevator were delighted to dispose of the empty corn cobs they accrued in shelling corn for their clients. Dad would back up to the holding bin and they would pull the rope and fill the wagon with cobs. The small building described above was used to store the cobs for later use to build fires in the winter time. The cobs made an excellent kindling if you kept them dry. Dad only used this method of obtaining fire starter for a couple years but the name, cob shed, stuck all of the remaining days we lived on the Shewman farm.

Most of the years the cob shed was used to store Dad's garden tools. Mother also made excellent use of the building to house hens that had "gone setting." This meant that some of the hens that we were keeping to lay eggs would, at the beckoning of nature, decide to raise a brood of chicks. Mother always seemed to be knowledgeable of just which eggs were fertile and which were not. She never bothered to explain this to me, and to this day I do not know how she was able to keep such details straight.

My nephews and I found that the north side of the cob shed made an excellent backstop when playing softball or baseball. Mom would place the selected eggs in a nest that was attached to the inside wall of the north side of the cob shed. The hen that had the "mothering notions" was placed on the nest. When my nephews and I played ball, and that was often, we would heave the ball with all of our strength against the side of the shed. This procedure didn't seem to obstruct the advancement of nature in hatching baby chicks. Mom marveled at the great results and never once asked Dad to move the nest to the other side of the building or for us to stop our use of the building as a backstop during hatching days.

In the process of hatching chicks from eggs, the eggs must be turned on a regular basis. I guess we did the turning for the hen and probably did a better job of it than the hen did.

Nephews and Other Fun Things

I think that I had the perfect opportunity offered to a small boy. I happened to be the last born of a family of seven. My oldest brother was twenty years my senior. My oldest sister was about eighteen years older than I. The children born to both of them were two to five years younger than I . What a perfect situation for playmates, to have Gene, Dean and Dale close to me in age.

Along with this closeness of age, we were able to be together at my house on many occasions. Gene lived about forty miles away. Dean and Dale lived on a series of farms in the Akron area or nearby neighborhoods. Gene's dad, my oldest brother, loved to fish. He fished every opportunity that he could. When he was not on the lake in a boat or on the river bank, he would be looking down through a hole in the ice no matter how cold it was.

Each and every weekend, as soon as the whistle blew at "Old Paranite Wire & Cable," my brother and his family headed north towards the Shewman farm. They would drop Gene off at my house. Forrest would then take his wife, Faun, and my niece, Namona, over to Faun's parents, about two miles east. Forrest would head straight to some lake he had been dreaming about all week. He might show up a time or two over the weekend for a bite to eat or he might not ever show until after dark on Sunday evening. He would come by and gather up his family and head back to Jonesboro and start planning for the next weekend. It has been said by plenty of people who knew Forrest that he was probably the most knowledgeable fisherman in Northern Indiana.

Dean, Billy, Doc the dog and Dale

With Gene at my house almost every weekend, there was lots of time to jump from one adventure to another. We would persuade my sister, Verna, to bring her boys, Dean and Dale, to spend the day. All of this provided a great time for us to really get acquainted. This set the stage for some of the greatest outdoor activities known to boys at that time. What we could not think of doing was probably not worth thinking of.

I was the oldest and Dale was the youngest. When teams were put together, Dale and I were one team. Gene and Dean were the other team. We would start playing softball or baseball early in the day and sometimes play all day. We would only take time out to eat and do other necessary functions. This is where the old cob shed building came into play. The shed became the silent member of each team, serving as the catcher. I usually pitched and played all of the bases as well as acting as a catcher to receive a throw from the outfield. Dale was my all purpose outfielder. Gene and Dean had a similar arrangement.

When we were in the midst of a great baseball game, young Dale's pride would often be injured. Dale would go in the house to see his grandmother, my mom. He would announce to her that we were cheating. He would say, "They cheat, they cheat."

Mom would say, "Now Dale, don't you worry. I'll make you a jelly bread and you can eat that." I have the picture well in mind of nephew, Dale, jelly bread in hand and mouth, looking out of the window on the north side of the kitchen. When the jelly bread had been devoured, out he would come ready to join in again. We had Dale filling in as a team member when he was very young. He could do a pretty good job of batting the ball when he was only five years of age.

The days that we were able to play together were many. The nephews seemed like brothers to me. Many times the four of us journeyed to the nearby swamps. Any wooded area or body of water, no matter how small it might be, was exciting to us. Wintertime would find us in the barn playing basketball or other creative games.

Some of the creative things seemed very important to me at the time. I was great on starting a new club. One of the first of these was one I labeled "the L.L. Club." This stood for "loose lion." For the life of me I do not to this day have the slightest idea of what I had in mind when I formed this club and gave it that odd name. I recall one of the special rituals and that was to go into the "privatist" of all private places, the three-holer, write the letters of the club name on a scrap of paper, light it with a match and drop in down the hole.

I suppose we were trying to do something just for boys and this was one way of doing it. Some of the clubs I started would have the trappings of small stars and badges that I was able to order from mail-order houses and the like. If I could have had access to some real funds I probably would have had something big going on.

**Billy (middle) with Dean and Dale.
Dixie Jewel is pulling the pony cart.**

Thousands of Firecrackers

My brother, Forrest, always seemed to know what little guys like us really wanted. One time he ordered a huge amount of fireworks from some place in Ohio. He told me that they cost over twenty-five dollars. That was a tremendous amount to spend on something that we were going to just burn up, but Forrest was that way. He never seemed to have thought for tomorrow but just saw the fun of today. Most of the time he arranged to participate in the pleasures he recognized as important for the "now" time.

Gene and I worked feverishly for days and days to set off all of the many kinds of fireworks . We would light entire packs of firecrackers and throw them out, pack after pack. We tried every trick in the book. I recall trying to send tin cans into orbit long before we knew what the word "orbit" meant. We even did weird inhumane things such as putting firecrackers in young sparrow's mouths. They were always in abundance on the Shewman farm. Life on the farm put the sparrow in a very lowly position. They destroyed and messed and were hated by most of the farmers of that time.

My first introduction to firecrackers was when I was about five or six. Mom would purchase a small pack of lady fingers for I believe about ten cents. That was it for several years, then the big purchase by Forrest. What a contrast! For my brother to spend what must have been the bigger part, if not all, of his weekly paycheck to make Gene and me happy was truly one of the high-water marks in our list of growing up experiences.

Let's Go Fishing

My dad did not fish much. The one and only time I remember Dad fishing he took me with him. I can almost see the old boat that we used, leaking water and us dipping it out at timely intervals. We did not have poles that were regulation. Dad made us a couple out of some long branches. We had real fish line and hooks and we always had red worms at our finger tips, for the ground around the barn where we piled manure was plentiful with them.

Dad had arranged with Frank, our neighbor, to use his boat on Little Summit Lake. Dad and I walked back through Frank's pasture fields and woods to the lake. The boat was old and had no oars. Dad used a pole for a paddle and out we went. We caught several blue-gills, a flat pan fish that in spite of its many bones is excellent eating. The ones we caught in those waters were about the size of a man's hand, perhaps as long as ten inches. I was about eight years old when this happened. I don't remember asking Dad to go fishing again. I really do not know why.

My other opportunities to fish were made possible by my brother Forrest. I went fishing with him through the ice on Lost Lake on January 2, 1938. The Christmas that was just a few days before was the occasion to receive my first diary. Forrest gave me the diary and I recorded our first ice fishing trip in it. The memories of ice fishing on Lost Lake in Wabash County are pleasant enough. But I can remember being a little frightened of the ice when I would hear it ripple with a splitting sound. Brother Forrest tried to reassure me that it was in fact freezing a little bit harder when it made that sound. It was difficult to stay warm on the ice. I had some trouble doing so.

But standing on some of the river banks in northern Indiana on a warm sunny day was an unequaled pleasure. Casting a hook out on the gently meandering Eel or the nostalgic Tippecanoe certainly was this small lad's favorite dream. Our fishing gear was usually very simple. We would tie a piece of fishing line to a small stick about four inches long and tie the other end to an old nail. This would make a fine stringer to place any fish that we might catch. Our river catches were usually goggle-eyes. Once in a while, we'd catch a perch or a catfish.

Most of the fun was just in being there. I would let my mind wander and imagine what it must have been like back in Indian days. I could almost see them fishing over on the other side of the river. Some of the area along the river banks was unspoiled, as I thought it must have been way back in Indian time. The time we had to spend on the rivers seemed to pass quickly. Long hours on the river encouraged the appetite very much and I usually became very hungry. My mom would send with us fried ham sandwiches that tasted out of this world to a couple hungry boys sitting on a river bank.

Going fishing with Forrest also meant that nephew Gene would go. We had many great times on the river. On several occasions we found fishing from a row boat in one of the nearby lakes to be very challenging. One time while fishing on nearby Flat Lake, Gene, attired in cutoff coveralls, sunburned his legs so badly that he couldn't sleep. He was in bad shape but he recovered after Mom greased him up with some of her favorite cures.

Other times in my early fishing career included fishing in a drainage ditch that ran through the farm share-cropped by my older sister and husband, Dean and Dale's parents. My nephews and I would use small hooks and drop them through the cracks of a bridge that crossed the ditch. The fish were small but fun to catch. If they were a little too large we would have to move them to the edge of the bridge and bring them up over the edge. This was sometimes a little tricky but we managed. We would keep Pepsi-Cola in the ditch to cool. My first drink of carbonated cola was there. I thought it was going to come out my nose.

Chicago Cubs Versus Me

I made up a game about baseball. I pretended that I was a one-man baseball team and that I would play the Chicago Cubs baseball team. I would listen to the games whenever we had a strong enough "B" battery on our radio to pull in the Chicago station, about one hundred miles distant. I knew all of the players, the positions they played and in what order they hit.

Behind the house was a lane, perhaps fifty feet in length, with a slight grade down to the county road below. The lane had many small pebbles and stones. I would use a board for a bat, toss up a stone with one hand, and swat the stone as far as I could over the orchard. I would do this by the hour, going through the entire Cubs roster for a full nine innings. I would let the Cubs get on base once in a while, but I usually pretended to catch everything that they hit to me.

When it was my turn to bat, I could not be put out. This contributed greatly to the long periods of time in finishing a game. The orchard and the pasture field beyond became covered with hundreds and hundreds of small rocks and pebbles that I would swat out day after day.

I found a small wooden baseball bat. I managed to beat the sides of the baseball bat down to where it was not much more than a mere thread of wood. I do not believe my dad ever caught on to what I was doing. He would probably have put a stop to all of the rocks being hit out into the orchard and pasture.

Making Hay and Rock Lake

Some of the hottest and dirtiest work on the farm was hay making. Dad mostly grew alfalfa. Alfalfa was a good cow feed, and horses also did nicely on it. We could get three separate cuttings each summer. The first cutting usually was the most productive.

Dad kept a close watch on the progress of the alfalfa and knew exactly when to cut it. He would use a two-horse team drawn mower. Much of my dad's time became involved in getting the mower ready to cut. The sickle bar was about four feet long and was made up of several triangle shaped cutting knives. This bar would slide back and forth in a track and cut the stems of the alfalfa. Dad would replace some of the knives from time to time. This required cutting off rivets and replacing the blades with new ones. Dad had a limited inventory of tools and consequently spent a lot of time in getting the mower ready to cut.

There came a day when Dad decided that enough was enough. Dad purchased a new McCormick-Deering mower. A farmer purchasing a new tool, in those days was similar to someone buying a new automobile today.

Dad would start on the outside edge of the field and go around and around, working his way towards the center of the field. I would watch the rabbits move towards the middle of the field as Dad got closer and closer to the elimination of all the stubble. Sometimes a snake would get in the way and the sickle bar would decide its fate in quick time.

The cut alfalfa would lay on the ground and the hot sun would beat down on it. If the sun cooperated nicely and the wind was blowing a little, the hay would cure in about two days. Dad would walk across the field and pick up a handful of hay here and there. He would select a certain stem and chew on it. He had the uncanny ability to know just exactly when the hay should be raked. This was the next procedure in hay making. If Dad had any question about the readiness of the hay, he would talk to my mom about it. Then they would go down to the field together and go through the same process of chewing on the stems. The amount of moisture or lack thereof determined the hay's readiness to "make."

Once Dad had decided that the hay was ready, out came the dump rake and old Charley the horse. I often wondered if the hay would have spoiled if my dad had not used the assistance of my mom. Not all crops and the decisions of what and when to do came with her blessing. Whether hay was ready to take in or not seemed to be her speciality.

Charley was a horse that could work by himself. Not all horses like to be put in between two wooden shafts and made to work alone. A dump rake had two wheels, two wooden shafts, a seat for the driver and a series of rakes or teeth shaped in half moons or half circles. The rake was about seven feet wide. The teeth dragged the hay up from the ground and gathered it into a round roll. If you were good in your timing, you would end up with long neat round rows of hay, about two feet high.

We would start the raking process after the morning dew had dried. Dad would only rake up what he thought we had time to take up before the hay started getting tough. If the day was long and hot, and a gentle breeze blowing, the hay could be brought in later in the afternoon, but not if it were cloudy. Hay left in a wind row could get rained on during the night. If you got caught in this kind of situation, about all you could do was be to turn the hay another time or two the next day, until it dried out.

We would eat an early lunch--dinner we then called it--and all the hands would head to the hay field. My first assignment, while yet small, was to perch myself

181

high up on the wagon rack just behind the horses and drive them from one row to the next. Someone would go ahead of the wagon and make paths through the raked rows of hay. This person would doodle up the hay into small piles on each side of the pathway. This made it easy for the ones on the ground to use their pitchforks to toss the hay up to my dad on the wagon. He worked the loading of the wagon, tramping down as much of the loose hay as he could. When I became trustworthy of using a three-tine pitch fork, I was appointed the "doodler."

It would take about thirty minutes to have a large enough load to please Dad and to the barn we would go. Dad would drive the horses and wagon up the slight grade into the right driveway of the barn. He would stop immediately under the middle, or ridge, of the barn. I recall Dad unhitching Charley and hooking him up to the hay rope.

When I was about four or five, I was given the important assignment of riding on top of Charley's old sweaty back. I would sit on his harness-covered back and drive him towards the road when I got the go ahead signal from Dad. We had a predetermined distance where I would stop, but I also would listen for Dad to yell, "whoa."

I would turn Charley around and return to the barn, being careful not to tangle the hay rope as we drug it back to the barn.

The hay rope was attached to a hay fork through a series of pulleys that pulled the hay fork full of hay up to the track located at the top of the barn. The fork would hit a carrier and run across the ridge of the barn and hover over the hay mow. Whoever was setting the hay fork would pull a trip rope attached to the fork, and the hay would dump into the mow. A couple of hot, thirsty brothers of mine would be waiting in the mow to put the hay evenly about the mow. We called this part of the process "mowing hay." Over and over this procedure was repeated until the wagon was empty. Then back to the field we would go for the next load.

When I was about ten, I traded the use of Charley for the old "thirty-three" family Ford V-8. This was a neat assignment for a ten year old. I would hook the hay rope to the front axle of the car. I could then view the pulling activity as I backed down the hill. When Dad gave me the signal, I would push in on the clutch peddle. The weight of the car would cause it to roll down the hill in front of the barn. At the right moment I would let out on the clutch and the car would start. This conserved on the use of the car battery. Car batteries in those days always seemed to be going down and would have to be taken to town to be recharged. I would watch for where my tracks were, stop the car, and drive the car back up the hill, straddling the rope as I returned to the barn. I would wait for my next signal from Dad and away I would go again.

I got pretty good at handling the car and would drive it anywhere I could. If I were anywhere around, Dad did not have to make any more trips to the barn to get the car. When a trip was mentioned, I would race ahead and start it up and bring it to the house.

We were always ready for Dad to call a halt to the day's hay making activities. We knew that as soon as the milking was finished we could head to Rock Lake for a refreshing swim and, of course, get our chance to wash off all of the dirt and dust of the day's work.

For a bathing suit, I used an old pair of bib-overalls that Mom had cut the pant legs off. The fashion craze you might expect today had not yet hit the Rock Lake community. You wore what you wanted and nobody paid the least bit of attention or expressed any opinion one way or the other.

The nickels and dimes that I earned working for the neighbors came in handy. I would use them to purchase ice-cold pop and perhaps a candy bar before hurrying home to a hot supper that Mom would have ready.

Our appetites in those days must have seemed fierce to our mom. Making hay was hard work and we used up a lot of energy. We would hit the supper table ready to eat like a horse. Mom would have fried some kind of pork meat. We had lots of ham in those days. She could make a good gravy. When placed over fresh hot corn bread, it was mouth watering. The evening meal was a good time to bring out all of the leftovers from the noon meal. When you are hungry, it all tastes good.

Most evenings after supper, on a hay making day, didn't include much storytelling. We were all very tired. On many occasions we knew that the next day would require us to get up and do it all over again.

"Ol' Tin Can"

During my junior high school days I started to become better acquainted with the boys in the neighborhood. On Sunday afternoons we would go over to the Saners' yard and play a game called "ol' tin can." There would be Lloyd, Bob and Roy Saner, Charles Landis, Dick and George Traver, Lester Eber and myself. We turned out to be quite a neighborhood mixture.

We would each select a stick to hit with and place a tin can on a block of wood. Someone would be elected to be "it" and the rest would run and hide. The ones hiding would start to slip back towards the tin can. They would hope that they would be able to sneak in and hit the tin can with their sticks and not be seen. If the one that was "it" saw the person coming, he would touch the can and call him out. The object of the game was to be as brave as you could when "it" and venture out, trying to catch sight of someone hiding. We played this until someone decided it was chore time. Then we would have to go home and do our various farm tasks.

Huckster, Orange Pop, Rock Lake
and Ice Cream

Any distance more than a mile was considered a trip and required the use of a sometimes temperamental automobile. World War II was on; gas was rationed and so were automobile tires. Each and every trip was planned out as much in advance as possible.

One way of helping to solve the farmer's shopping plight was in the appearance of the huckster truck. Some enterprising merchant in one of the nearby hamlets would decide to take his store to the country. One such storekeeper used a ton and a half stake truck with a covered bed. The truck had shelves along each side and on the end behind the cab, and a full grown adult could stand up inside it. The storekeeper would stock the truck with the most essential groceries.

The truck would stop in front of the house on the edge of the road under the pear trees. He would open up the big doors, pull out the step up box and by this time Mom and I would be ready to climb up into the enchanting atmosphere. What fun to see all of the many items stacked in neat rows just like in the store. Mom usually had eggs from her hens that she would trade out to the

Huckster Man for staple items of everyday use in her kitchen. Mother called this fund her "egg money." She knew full well that she had to make it last. These funds had to meet the day to day necessities of the children living at home.

These were the early days of the "Watkins Man." Mother would purchase an orange extract from him and it made the best "orange pop." I would go to the well house and pump the water off until it became very cool. I would then go to the barn and browse through the straw mow until I would find a straw that had a long distance between the joints. I would snip the straw at the joints with Mom's shears and would come up with a very usable pop straw. It would be almost as good as one I would get at the store at Rock Lake.

When I could manage to save up a nickel, I would get on my old trusty bike and head for Rock Lake. I would ride the mile plus distance to the lake, and if it were before supper, I would stop on the way at Roy Landis's house. Roy owned property that bordered the lake. He did some farming and ran a refreshment stand at the lake. Roy never quizzed me on how much money I was going to spend. He would stop whatever he was doing and go down and open up the store just for little old me. The very most I would spend would be ten cents.

I would sit and sip my orange drink and try to carry on big guy fishing talk with Roy. I would ask him all of those important questions about how the fish were biting and on what kind of bait. Roy would pocket my nickel and never let on that he might be concerned in the least that this little farm boy had disturbed his afternoon activity. On those few rare occasions, a large nickel "Powers" candy bar went very well with my pop.

Roy also had another interesting business project. Most of the Indiana winters were cold enough to freeze over Rock Lake to as much as a foot thick. Roy would saw out blocks of ice about a foot square. He would get a huge load of saw dust from the local saw mill and pack the ice in the saw dust in his ice house. The ice would last until the early part of the summer. The large blocks would become substantially smaller as the summer progressed.

We would purchase a block of ice from Roy every so often and make homemade ice cream with it. I have many fond memories of the large two-gallon green wooden freezer. The milk house made a great place to crush the ice on the cement floor. It also provided shade and a cooler place than other locations we might have used. Lots of stories were spun around the milk house while we were making ice cream.

Mother and my sister, Verna, would cook the special skimmed cream from the top of the milk can, along with sugar and the secret ingredient, junket tablets. I was convinced that one had to put those tablets in the mix or the end product would not be nearly as good.

Out to the milk house the mix would come, still warm but soon to be cooled in the freshly smashed ice packed freezer. We would all take turns turning the handle to the freezer, the smaller ones of us going first while the turning was easier. Dad usually had the assignment of being the last one. With his big strong hands and farm-hardened arms, he could determine almost without fail when the ice cream was ready.

Mom would show up about this time in the process and remove the paddle, placing it on a plate she had brought with her. One of the older brothers usually received the honor of cleaning the paddle. The rest of us had to watch Dad place the remaining ice in the gunny sack that it had been crushed in and pack it around the top of the freezer. Dad was again the one who said, "OK, lets eat." My, what good-tasting fun came out of that old green two-gallon wooden bucket.

No matter how many hot, hungry mouths were around, we always seemed to have enough to satisfy all.

There were special occasions when money was appropriated for the purpose of purchasing a block of ice from Roy Landis for the kitchen icebox. Most of the time the icebox stood as a large oversized end-table in the kitchen.

**Rock Lake, the summer swimming hole.
Note the model T Ford cars. One was probably ours.**

8

FAMILY FRUGALITY

Please, Mom, Just Mustard

During the first couple of years of grade school I carried a small lunch pail. It was an oblong tin container, sort of a funny shaped small bucket. It was considered vogue to carry a pail during the early years. However, I soon fell into the age-old trap of doing what the rest of the gang did. In this situation, they started carrying their lunches in throw away lunch bags. Mine was usually wrapped in newspaper. Mom would put two sausage sandwiches and sometimes an apple in my lunch pail.

A sausage sandwich is very tasty if you can eat it while it is still warm. After a sausage sandwich has been in your lunch pail and out in the hall for about four hours in pretty cold weather, it is terrible tasting. The grease starts to form into white lard and you find that it becomes very difficult to force down.

For a change, my mom would make for me a scrambled egg and mustard sandwich. She fried the egg, scrambled it and then stirred an ample quantity of mustard into it. After so much of this sort of thing, I became bored with eating so many eggs. I asked Mom, "Can't you just leave the eggs out and put just mustard on the bread?" She did, and that is the way it came through, just mustard and bread.

Mom found a place where she could get fresh ground peanut butter. I can still see that oblong dish with ridges all around the bottom side and a lid to keep the contents fresh. I think it must have held a pound or so. When I reached the point of boredom of "just mustard", she started making peanut butter sandwiches.

Cold Packing, Brown Sugar, Pepper and Old Newspapers

Life in the Depression years was one of trying to survive. Living on a farm made it easy to have a large garden. I remember my dad spending long hours in the field, coming to the barn, unharnessing the horses and feeding them. Then he got all of the milking equipment ready and took it to the barn. Next, he would let the cows in and feed them. Milking came next and all of the straining, cooling and equipment cleanup.

You would think that after a long day in the field, bouncing around on all of the rocks that were so commonplace on the Shewman farm, Dad would be worn out. He was, but he still would spend the balance of the daylight hours working in the garden hoeing and pulling weeds. The garden was very close to the road and Dad wanted to make sure that there were no weeds for neighbors to view as they passed by on their way to Akron.

Mother had what seemed like an endless supply of Ball and Kerr glass fruit jars. I know that Mom also knew she had a good supply of them, and, as it seemed to me, she tried her best to fill them all with whatever she could glean from the garden or find money to purchase

195

elsewhere. One of my tasks, after I grew big enough to be trusted with them, was to carry the jars down the cellar steps and place them on the cement ledge at the east end of the cellar.

We always butchered at least one hog each fall. Fall of the year was an easier time to work with the meat. A good cold frosty morning kept the meat fresher, and besides that it was nice and cozy to stand around the big fire burning under the big black butchering kettle. Dad would fill the kettle with water to use in scrapping and cleaning the hog of all of its hair.

I never did like to watch the actual killing of the hog when I was small. I just remember hearing the rifle crack down in the hog lot. The next thing I knew, I could see Dad drag the hog up to the orchard with the help of Charley, the good old faithful horse. Much of the time Dad would ask George Kreig, a neighbor that lived about a mile south of us, to help butcher. George had a good reputation of cooking off cracklings that would make the purest and whitest of lard when rendered.

After the hog had been shot and dragged to the orchard area, it was rolled onto a platform made of some odds and ends of boards. A barrel was tilted at one end of the platform, allowing several available strong arms to push the hog in and out the barrel that had been filled with the scalding water. Up and down the ones doing the work would move the hog, with periods in between of scrapping hair from the skin. This was always a dirty, smelly job, but was necessary to get the hog ready to butcher. Three poles were positioned nearby with heavy duty hooks secured to the upper part of the poles. The hog's legs were slit in such a fashion to allow the hooks to be placed in the slits and pushed to an upright position. With the hog suspended in this position it was easy to slit it open, finish the draining of the blood and start the carving of parts and interior cleaning. Nothing was wasted or tossed. Dad used it all. Some neighbors said that Dad saved everything but the pig's squeal and he would save it if he knew of a way to can it up.

The actual process of curing the hams and shoulders was an exciting event. Dad would spread newspapers that had been collected from the neighbors and my sister, Verna, all over the kitchen table. Once they got started, I would stand around making sure that I kept out of the way, watching with great anxiety the various steps and procedures that Dad and Mom went through to start the process of curing meat.

I remember the ingredients Dad and Mom used in the curing process. There was salt, black pepper, red pepper and, of course, brown sugar. The brown sugar stands out the most in my memory of all of the ingredients. It caught my attention just as soon as it hit the table for curing use. This was an annual event and my dad made sure that I could have a few lumps of this delicious sweet treat for my very own. I would stand back eagerly waiting for the first lump while watching the curing process

Dad gently rolled the hams and shoulder meats about, pressing a mixture of the salt, peppers and sugar into the meat. What the process actually did, I never did know. He was a master in curing meat and knew just how long to continue this process of rubbing and rolling the meats around on the kitchen table. When Dad thought he had used his magical hands enough, he would wrap the pieces of meat in the available newspaper. Mom would have bleached a sufficient quantity of old feed sacks to where they looked almost white. Into these bleached feed sacks they would stuff the newspaper wrapped hams and shoulder meats.

Since the butchering process was done in cold weather, storing the meats while curing was an easy process. The feed sacks were tied with binder twine that was always available on the farm and suspended on strings from nails driven into the rafters of the meat house building. The meat had to be hung away from the interest of the rats and mice that were in abundance on the Shewman farm. We would wait for some time to pass. I never did learn just how many days Dad wanted the meat to hang and cure. Sausage would be stuffed direct from the grinder into cleaned hog intestines or, as Mom did in later years, tube-shaped cloths she had sewn together. After the sausage had hung overnight in the meat house it became as hard as rock. Mom would go out and cut off a hunk and bring it back into the kitchen and slice it in about one-half inch thick patties. What a treat to have this fresh sausage with fried fresh eggs from our own hen house.

Saving Apples Dad's Way

Another trick I saw my dad do concerned apples. We had what I thought was a nice orchard, ample in most years to yield sufficient fruit for our family to use during the winter. There were about four kinds of apples in the orchard. Most people would pick apples when they were ripe and put them in their cellar. This would be fine for a while.

Apples didn't last long in the cellar. Some of the apples would start to rot. Again I thought my dad to be super smart in all kinds of things. Dad had ways of excelling in ideas that allowed his family to live a good life in spite of the meager means he had about him. Dad decided to dig a hole in the orchard ground, about five feet deep and five feet square. He filled the hole about a third of the way up with wheat straw from the barn. The ripe apples were carefully placed in the straw up to about two feet of the ground level. Dad filled up the hole with more wheat straw and covered it with about a foot of dirt.

When we wanted apples to eat, Dad would remember the apples in the hole in the ground out in the orchard. Some of the time I would trek along with him, carrying our coal-oil lantern, shovel and a small pan for the apples. Dad would proceed to open the hole. Sometimes this was quite a chore. The cold Indiana nights would have the ground frozen so hard that Dad would have to get the grubbing hoe, a large, heavy-duty, pick-type tool. Dad would take the grubbing hoe and break the ground loose. Sure enough, the apples were there nestled in the straw, cold to the touch but usually not frozen.

I reminisce very fondly upon this event and can almost taste the delicious cold apples that we munched, accompanied sometimes by fresh popped pop-corn. We would sit around the living room Rayboy heating stove, basking in our good fortune and never fully realizing that this was just a simple feast. What we did realize was that the heat from the stove and juice from the apples helped move us through the fore part of the evening and made the cold wintry Indiana nights much more bearable.

Beans and More Beans

Corn was not always planted by itself in the fields. Sometimes we planted green pole beans along beside the stalk. The stalk of corn made an excellent pole for the bean to vine upon. Mom declared that there was only one kind of bean to plant in the corn field--Kentucky Wonder Bean. They not only made an excellent table food while fresh but were also excellent canned. They helped fill up the hundreds of fruit jars that my mom had and dedicated herself to filling.

Mom used a process in canning that she called "cold packing." Vegetables were packed in jars and boiled in water for a prescribed period of time. When the snow was flying and Mom's nice warm kitchen smelled of her good cooking, all the bean planting, picking, canning and lugging of the full jars to the cellar, plus the work that this created, seemed very worthwhile even to this small farm lad.

Soup beans were another important crop for winter consumption. Dad and Mom planted the Great Northern variety. When the beans had matured they would be pulled up stalk and all and brought to the barn. We had an empty wagon box that I never saw used but for this one purpose, and that was to shell the soup beans in. After placing the bean stalks in the wagon box, they would be beaten, stomped on and kicked about in any fashion that would break the pod hull and allow the bean to be free. As a little fellow my task often was to become the "thrasher."

After taking the vines and any loose trash out of the wagon box, we would sweep up the shelled beans and chaff and put them into buckets. I can see my mom standing on the hill in front of the barn, sifting the beans from one bucket to the other. She seemed to know when the wind was going to blow a little extra strong, because that would be the day she would choose to shell beans. The beans went from bucket to bucket until Mom was satisfied that it was as good as she was going to get them.

Before Mom could cook the beans, she spent considerable time picking through them, dumped in that famous lap apron of hers. When she was satisfied they were ready for the stove, she proceeded in their preparation, using a recipe that was out of this world. Nothing could beat some of Mom's soup beans, cornbread and sliced onion on a cold winter's day. Come to think of it, they tasted pretty good in the summer also.

The Huckleberry Swamp

There was an area just west of the Shewman farm barn that had lots of huckleberry bushes. There were also several trees spaced among the bushes. When the spring rains came there would be water left standing in parts of the huckleberry bush area. Low ground areas that had water standing in them were called marshes or swamps. Lots of berries would be available each summer. I can remember people coming from all parts of the area to share-pick them. If we sold them outright we would share the monies received with Mr. Shewman, the landlord. A good many of the pickers would pick on shares. We only had to share the cash received with Mr. Shewman. This would leave a lot of berries on hand for my mom to can. And can she did. Here was another opportunity for her to engage in what she considered an important life assignment of hers: to fill the fruit jars. All of this farm excitement supplied an opportunity for me to see strangers and become a little more familiar with how the rest of the world ticked.

Let's Shoo the Flies, Billy

Life on the farm with lots of hogs, cattle, and horses meant flies. The common house fly would be present all of the warm weather times and was always trying to get into the house. I would see hundreds matted on the screen door to the wash room. They were just waiting for someone to open the screen door so they could rush in. I suppose the good smells of Mom's kitchen drew them in. The ceiling of the kitchen would almost look black with hundreds of them sitting there waiting to drop down onto someone's plate of food.

Everyone learned the tricks to somewhat limit the mass accumulation of the pesky critters. If you jiggled the screen door or gently slammed it in and out before entering it would get many of them buzzing in the air while you quickly jumped into the house.

Many afternoons, after flies had entered and lodged themselves on the kitchen ceiling, we had another exercise in which I played a vital part. I call this exercise, "Let's shoo the flies, Billy." My mother and my sister, Christeen, if she were present, would take dish towels and start in the far corner of the kitchen from the outside door. They would start shooing the flies towards the door. My job was to be ready, and at the right time, quickly open the door while huge swarms of flies escaped the rush and swish of dish towels. This exercise would then be repeated until Mom was satisfied that it was about as good a job as they could do. We never did get all of them out at any one given time. It always looked to me as if there were still hundreds left to pester us when we ate. I remember watching the flies swoop in and out of Dad's open mouth as he would take a nap during a hot summer's noon break. I thought it to be great sport to listen to the hum of the fly as it zoomed about in the hollow cavernous area of Dad's mouth.

When we thought that we had all of the flies on the outside I would go out, armed with whatever kind of fly swatter was available, and start swatting the hundreds of flies now on the outside of the door.

The All Important Three-holer
Wow--1000
Sheets

Probably the most private place on the farm was the conspicuous looking building that stood at the end of a well worn trail at the edge of the orchard. We fondly referred to this building as the "three-holer." In other words, it was the "country john." This facility worked just fine in the summer. Well, not exactly just fine. There were times when the aroma and the presence of flies could be a little distracting and sometimes more than objectionable.

When the weather started producing snow, and the extremely cold temperatures well known to Indiana hit, the path through the snow did not show as much activity as it did when it was flanked by grass. This quite often became a factor in a person becoming constipated. I learned early on to use the school house facilities as late in the day as I could, and then be ready for an early trip to the school house john just as soon as I arrived at school the next morning.

One of the nasty tricks we young boys would pull was to catch someone in the "john" and then throw rocks against the building. When you are cooped up in such a small area, and rocks come banking off the outside walls, the shock and sound can be very loud and very objectionable. My sister, Christeen, and others can verify these happenings. Mother would hear about our thoughtless acts and we sure got a talking to. This was great sport for me and my nephews.

Over the years of observing the activity of this very private building, I can testify that one of the better uses of the Sears and Roebuck catalog was demonstrated in this facility. There just cannot be any rougher way to complete nature's daily call than with paper from a catalog. Unless, of course, you were one of the rough and tough farmers who would use an empty corn cob. There were some that handled their daily function in this manner, usually at the barn where they found they had little or no time to make the journey to the wooden john.

One day when I was quite small, Dad came back from his usual weekly shopping trip to Dan Leininger's General Store. It seems that he had discovered a new product that the Leiningers were pushing--toilet paper. When Dad read the bold inscription on the label that proudly declared that there were one thousand sheets in the roll, he became very excited. Dad thought the label said that it could handle the paper work for a "thousand shits." I remember both Mom and Dad laughing.

Dad knew that we would need something to unwind the paper from the roll, so he made a very nice wooden toilet paper holder and mounted it on the wall of the three-holer. Again, Dad proved that he could adapt to the world and was able to practice some more of his make-do contributions to our daily comfort.

It seems like only yesterday that I was sitting in this little building, intent on my reason for being there but also tuned in on the sounds nearby; of the birds chirping, bees buzzing and even the pesky mosquitoes nipping at my bottom side, all happily doing what they do best.

Christmas On the Farm

All of our Christmas times could be described as meager. We would get a tree in town, one cut some-place else, dry and brittle,for fifteen cents. Mom would save shiny things from year to year to put on it. Once in awhile she would buy a box of sparkly icicles for ten cents. Christeen and Irvin, would string up bright red cord rope from one corner of the dining room to the other. Mom had a couple of red bells in her inventory of

Christmas decorations. She would tie them to the red rope to dangle in the middle of the room. This always seemed to add cheer to the long cold winter evenings as we sat around the stove, waiting for Christmas to come.

Santa was always a part of my Christmas. The older ones of the household would warn me that Santa might spit tobacco juice in my eyes if I stayed up too late on Christmas Eve. My dad chewed tobacco. I was convinced that somewhere in the magic of Christmas time, my little stocking would have something very wonderful in it. I always hoped that wonderful thing would be so large that it would have to rest on the floor beside the sock. Most of the little notes that I pinned to my stocking would read, "Dear Santa, please bring me what you think is best."

I was viewing Christmas in the dark Depression days and I was coached by my older brothers and sister to leave it up to Santa to decide. After all, Santa did know best in what could be afforded.

On one occasion, a little carpenter set showed up. I was told that it cost fifty cents. I took it to school for show and tell. It had a saw, small hammer and a ruler. I stood up and proudly said, "This cost fifty cents." Later, I realized that the more affluent kids must have made fun of me.

My mother would try to do something for all of the grandchildren. The number varied upwards to seven during my growing up years. She would usually buy a nickel hanky for each. No one complained; we had lots of fun, a big Christmas dinner, and lots of love around our sparkly tree every year.

It was also the custom of our school hack driver to give us each an orange, an apple, a candy cane, and occasionally a candy bar. I longed for the afternoon that introduced the Christmas holiday. Many years, that orange was the only one I would get all year long.

When the Wall Paper Gets Dirty

All clean things in time get dirty. Every so often it was time to clean the wall paper. Burning coal for heat created lots of smoke and soot every time the stove doors were opened. Careful as you might be, the walls would show the dirt.

Each spring Dad and Mom would talk about the situation and decide if we could afford to get some cleaner.

Dan Leininger's general store carried a brand called Climax. The cleaner was sealed in a can and came in one big hunk about three inches round and three inches high. The cleaner was pink in color when it came out of the can and resembled bubble gum. Mom would cut the hunk into two pieces. Whoever was doing the cleaning would knead the piece given to them until it became soft and pliable. Then all one had to do was to start at the top of the wall and drag the cleaner smoothly and evenly down the paper for about two feet, then stop and knead the dirt gathered into the cleaner. This process went on until the cleaner became so full of dirt that it took on a grey-blue look and you were convinced that it had absorbed all of the dirt that it was going to take in. We used to think that this method was a pretty good way and that it did a very good job.

Bittersweet, Candy, and the Man From Chicago

The fence that ran along the road next to the northern most field of the Shewman farm had a bittersweet berry vine clinging to it. Not much attention was paid to this vine during most of the year, but when fall came, the berries ripened into a beautiful shade of orange. As far back as I can remember, there would be some men from Chicago who stopped by to talk to my mother about harvesting the berries. They always came several days before harvest time and brought a box of candy with them which they very ceremoniously gave to Mom. Later,they returned and proceeded to harvest the orange berries. They would pay my mother a few dollars for them. This windfall of cash really came in handy.

Mother always had projects that needed money, and she did not have too many ways of obtaining the funds. My sister, Christeen, had at least one good memory of this berry event. She needed some new clothes for a particular school event and the timing of the berry sale was perfect. The men who bought the berries took them to the big city and multiplied their investment many times. The berries lasted way into the winter and added great looking color to any room the purchaser wanted to decorate.

The Garden and the Grindstone

Summertime and the eating of the fruits of the garden were an experience in itself. Dad and Mom were real experts in raising vegetables. Dad would to do all of the heavy work, such as getting the ground ready, plowing, harrowing, laying out the rows, and doing the hilling-up work. What Dad was really adamant about was his unremitting attack on the weeds. It was a good thing that the summer days were long. Dad needed all the time he could get. He would work the fields all day long. By seven o'clock he would have milked the cows and eaten supper. Then he would go to the garden and hoe and hand cultivate with a small garden plow until it was too dark to see any longer.

I could never understand how Mom would know when to look for small potatoes. I couldn't see them, for they were under the ground. On just the right day, she would instruct me to carefully dig around the roots of the new potato plants and remove some of the small tender potatoes. Her expression of this act was to "gravel out." This expression would only apply to the first new potatoes of the season. After the potatoes were larger or mature, we would "dig" them.

213

Mom had the green peas timed to start maturing at the same time that the small new potatoes were coming on. She mixed the peas and the new potatoes into a very delicious dish.

Mother would go out to the side of the road where she was sure that no one had tramped and where it was not very likely that man or beast had answered the call of mother nature. There she would find fresh dandelion greens. Mother had a recipe she held to that was so tasty. When we had new potatoes, new peas, and added fresh dandelion greens, we were really eating high. When I was very small, I did not like this bill of fare. But as I grew older, my tastes changed and I became very fond of this type of eating. All of this was very good for us. The only thing that we probably over-did was the sweets. My parents thought that it was critical to always keep a supply of sugar on hand. They would even buy it in large bags. Mother would make pies or cobblers or, from time to time, cakes. She did not spare on the use of sugar in making all of these goodies.

I remember some very healthy rhubarb stalks that grew along the west side of the garden next to the highway. Some called it pie plant. I would call it "plow point" when I was little and learning how to talk. I had heard Dad talk about doing something to the plow point on his plow.

Mom made a cobbler from the rhubarb stalk that was very good. She had to puts lots of sugar in it to remove some of the tart taste. We ate lots of the rhubarb from the stalks along the highway garden fence. But it always grew back and kept us in a bountiful supply.

The plow point was the removable point of the breaking plow shovel. It was removable in order to sharpen it from time to time. If you were affluent you would take the plow point into town and have someone sharpen it for you. This was out of the question in our case. We had a grindstone. It was usually located at the edge of the orchard under a tree for shade. Dad would suspend a rusty old tin can with a small nail hole in the bottom from a limb of a tree. He would position the grindstone under the can so that when water was placed in the can it would drip on the wheel.

The grindstone wheel was mounted in a treadle-type machine. He would stand at the wheel holding various parts of farm equipment that needed sharpening and pedal away. The water would drip on the wheel and make for better sharpening. I still have an image of Dad, an old dirty, sweaty straw hat perched on his heavily whiskered, sun tanned head, peddling away.

Corn, the Main Thing

To a farmer living in Northern Indiana during the Great Depression, a good corn crop was the only thing he could really count on to help get the family through those very hard times.

Corn could be ground and fed to the milk cows. Corn could and was fed to the hogs. Corn was fed to the chickens. On many occasions we took hand picked ears of corn to Halderman and Baum's feed elevator in Akron and had them fine cracked into corn meal. What delicious bread my mom would make from this home grown meal.

Many times I would dip fresh milk from a can in the milk house. The milk would still be warm, fresh from the cows only minutes before. I would place a couple of quarts into a small aluminum kettle that we used just for such occasions. I would take the milk to the house, and we would put fresh baked corn bread into a glass of this partially cooled milk. It sure tasted good. I did not have much trouble making an entire meal out of this delicious treat.

216

The Old Well house
and Milk House

Two of the more important buildings on the farm were the milk house and the well (pump) house. These two buildings were side by side, separated by about three feet. As fresh cool water was pumped from the well house, it ran through a pipe into the cement pit in the milk house. After milking had been completed, the milk was brought to the milk house. Then we proceeded to pour the milk through a strainer sitting on top of an eight-gallon can. A new cotton pad was placed in the strainer each milking time. The pad would catch any dirt or flies that might have gotten into the milk somewhere between the cow's teat and the delivery to the milk house. The stray dog, Shep, that came to live with us would eat the strainer pads after we pitched them out the milk house door. He would be waiting and sometimes would catch them in the air. I would find evidence of the strainer pad around the outside area of the milk house where old Shep had made his daily deposits.

The milk can was placed in the cool water in the cement pit. Before Dad's stirrer invention, we had to sit on the edge of the water pit and stir the warm milk by hand. Stirring hastened the cooling of the milk. This was a boring task. Again my dad came to the front with an idea. He watched the pump jack going up and down as it pumped water and decided to use some of the lost motion. He attached a piece of cord to the top of the pump jack and threaded it through some holes he made in the walls of the well house and milk house. He made a wooden frame and mounted it directly over the milk cans with hinges fastened to the milk house wall. The frame provided a good spot for Dad to install a couple of snaps for the stirrer handles to hook into.

When the pump jack went up and down it moved the string. The string was attached to the frame with the stirrers and took over the boring task of stirring the milk. What a relief! It would stir the milk as the pump jack went up and down pumping fresh cool water to the water tank for the livestock. It was a brilliant invention. I remember more than one curious soul watching this work with much amazement. My dad had many ingenious thoughts and inventions, and he only had a third grade education.

The cord wore out quickly but that did not stop my dad. He cut long leather laces from pieces of old harness leather he had on hand. The laces lasted for a much longer period of time as they passed through the complex series of pulleys.

The Author revisits the old Shewman farm.

The Author revisits the old well house where "Fritz" had "his" kittens and Dad invented a new way to stir milk.

9

CHURCH STUFF

Shake the Building, Lord

My earliest memory of church goes back to about age three. There was a small log building, just east of Rock Lake, known to all as the Log Bethel Church of God. I remember my mother teaching my class of two and three year olds. Our class would meet in the front part of the building, an area sometimes referred to as the amen corner. Mother was a good teacher. I appreciate all of the good instruction I received in Sunday School from her and also at home.

There was a story about this particular church in its earlier existence. The story was told from time to time in

221

my presence and I believe it to be true. As the story goes, the local minister of the church was in the practice of praying very loudly. Quite often he would call on the Lord to "shake this building."

The local big boys of the neighborhood heard about this loud praying and stopped by to confirm what they had heard. Obviously, they did their listening from outside the building. These normal, mischievous young boys left the church yard, knowing full well they would return. They had heard the minister call on the Lord for action to prove a point with his congregation.

The church was not on a cement foundation. The carefree boys returned the next night of service and waited outside the building with long poles they had located. When the minister got into his usual prayer and in his lifted voice said, "Lord, if you are with us, shake this building," the young men were ready with their poles placed under the corners of the log building. Now, some of these young men were very strong. I later knew some of the boys as full grown adults. They were very capable for this assignment. As the story goes, the boys really rocked the building and made believers quickly of those inside. As of this writing, the church building is still located at the same spot. Many changes have been made and it no longer looks like the little log church that I attended.

222

Bible Belt Bible School

Northern Indiana is right in the middle of what some people refer to as the Bible Belt. The town of Akron with its three churches had a listed population at that time of 996 residents. You would think that with three churches attendance at each would be small. On the contrary, the Church of God had around 400 people that called it home on Sundays. The Methodist Church and the Brethren Church had a large following as well. This did not mean that all of Akron's inhabitants were church goers. Many farmers drove considerable distance, maybe up to five or six miles, to do their worshiping.

After a few years at the Log Bethel Church, my parents decided to start attending the Akron Church of God. Most people in the area went to church. When school was out in the spring, the three church pastors got their heads together and formed a Vacation Bible School.

Since the Akron Church of God was the largest church in town, they usually had the most to say in what went on in the Bible school. I can remember Rev. D.L. Slaybaugh having most of the assignments in teaching. There was a blind man who played the accordion who would come and play his instrument and lead us through some choruses. The name of the blind man was Oscar Wilde. This man without sight could play such pretty melodies and to a young farm lad it made a lasting impression.

The vacation Bible school only lasted for two weeks. The Bible school was just in the mornings. The local grade school building was made available since practically every tax paying resident in the area likely had a participant in the event. We had a long recess time to play ball. I thought that was great stuff to get to use skills I was starting to pick up during regular school recesses and noon hours.

I think a lot about this annual summer event and remember with much gratitude the local church people who gave of their time to help start some of us down the right road, perhaps helping just a little bit to straighten some of the kinks for some of us. One of these farmers was John Gerig. John would take time out of his busy spring farm work to partake in our class instruction and at play time, play softball with us. I know that it was people like John that kept the fabric of this great country real and true. This was not only what the founding fathers intended to be, but I also believe the good Lord smiled down on such warm and memorable activities. Those summers rank high in my list of worthwhile times spent in growing up.

A short time later, when I was about twelve years of age, I recall helping John and his wife Selina. They taught a junior church for young children as a part of the Akron Church of God. Another young lad, Dick Higgins, also helped in this effort. We became good buddies and later got together in the South Pacific during World War II.

The Road Block and Church

By the time I was twelve years old, I could drive the "thirty-three" as good as anyone. My mother knew this and was very comfortable with me driving her to town and to church. On a lot of Sunday mornings it would be just the two of us making the trip into Akron. One Sunday morning as Mom and I approached the little town of Akron, we noticed a state police car parked across the road. Mom got very nervous. Estel Bemenderfer, the area state police officer, came up to the window. By this time my mom was praying up a storm. It worked. The officer smiled very nicely and asked me if I had seen such and such a car on our way into town. I swelled up as much as I could to look as big as possible for a twelve year old boy. I was aware that the officer knew that this little farm boy was taking his mother to church at this time on a Sunday morning. He was not about to give me a ticket, even though I didn't look old enough to be driving or have a legal driving license.

In a small community like Akron, almost everyone was known to one another. We knew each other's position in the community and had mutual respect for the rights of others. As long as no harm was being done, life was allowed to continue.

Dinner on the Ground

For Years the Church of God has had a campground located on the shores of Yellow Lake in Northern Indiana. For me camp meeting was a time of summer fun and picnics. We came to the grounds by auto, but I recall seeing horses and buggies and horse drawn wagons tied to some of the many shade trees.

I could hardly wait for church to let out at noon. This meant Mom had brought with her some of her specialty picnic foods to eat. Always there was fried

226

chicken. This was the special event of the year and I could depend on having pork and beans right out of the can. What a treat! This occasion found bananas on the quilt that Mom had spread on the ground. We might not see another banana the rest of the year, but this summer outing was extra special.

I would play hooky from church services and spend most of my time along the shoreline of Yellow Lake, skipping stones with my friend, Dick Higgins. I went to some of the services, those that Mom insisted I attend.

Some of the years, a man with a small airplane would land in the pasture field close by and take people for a ride. How I would have liked to go up in the sky like a bird. I remember the cost to be fifty-cents. Dad and I would watch all of the takeoffs and landings. We never had the opportunity to take a ride. Dad said that was too much for too little in hard times.

Dad helping Frank build his new barn.
I would know that hand on that hip anywhere.

10

FUN AT FRANK'S

Something about Frank

Of all of the neighbors in the Summit neighborhood, I remember Frank Royer the best. I spent many hours with Frank, some social, but most as his employee. Frank lived across the huckleberry swamp. He was the son of Vinee and when she died he took over the farm.

If one were going to see Frank by vehicle, it meant approaching his place by the means of a long lane which was always full of chuck holes. Some times they were filled with mud and water and they were always rough and bumpy. I rarely ever drove a car down this lane, but I certainly went down it plenty of times on my flimsy ol' bike.

My first experience of using this lane was to deliver magazines to Frank. I was using my first bike, with its twenty-eight inch high-pressured tires glued onto the rims. Quite often the glue would separate when I would ride the bike through the water puddles in Frank's lane. This meant that I would have to reglue the tire back onto the bicycle rim.

I became involved in selling magazines when I was ten years old. I had yet another young boy's wild dream. I thought that I could become rich in this kind of a project. After all, Frank had said he would take the Colliers magazine. I could sell the magazine to him for five cents, send three and one-half cents to the publisher, and I would have an entire cent and a half to keep. On one occasion I caught Frank a little short on cash. He gave me two pennies and a three cent stamp. It worked out just fine with me, for I needed a postage stamp to mail my collections to the publisher.

Each time I would have to put the bike tire back on after submerging them in Frank's mud puddles, I would remind myself of this enterprise that I was engaged in. This kept me going. I think often about this business venture. Today I compare these pennies with the couple of dollars that I leave on the table for a waitress that I do not even know.

"Keep the Hell out"

There was a time that Frank had a sign posted in a small parcel of land in the front yard of his house. Frank had planted alfalfa in this small parcel. At the very beginning, guests or visitors coming to see Frank would pull up into the alfalfa with their cars. Frank did not like this and took care of it by posting a sign. The sign read,"Keep the Hell Out of My Alfalfa." Mother could not handle this kind of language and did not like to pass in front of the sign. She would go out of her way to avoid it, and if she knew it were in view, would turn her head the other way.

Working for Frank

My first assignment on Frank's farm was to help plant potatoes. Frank cut the tongue out of a horse-drawn potato planter and put a short tongue in to use with his tractor. I would sit in the planter seat and watch, making

231

sure that a piece of potato would be on every knife of the planting wheel as it came around. I could do this task as soon as I was big enough to sit on the seat without falling off. The danger of falling was very minimal because of the soft muck earth and the unlikelihood of the wheel hitting a bump.

Frank owned a small Allis-Chalmers tractor. It was not long before Frank had me breaking ground with a fourteen-inch single-bottom plow mounted on the tractor. From this I went to getting all of the usual assignments that went with farming at that time.

Frank would pay me about twenty-five cents per hour at the beginning of my working for him. He increased this to thirty-five cents before I graduated from high school and left his employment to go into the U.S. Navy. Part of my pay was lunch. At twelve o'clock sharp, Frank and I would stop what we were doing. Usually we were at the house end of the field row when we stopped.

Frank had a large gray enamel ware coffee pot. Frank would add more coffee grounds to what was already in the pot, fill the pot with water and put it on the stove to boil. The only time the grounds came out of the pot would be when there was no room for water to be added. Then only part of the grounds were dumped. Frank never washed the pot. After Frank got married, I wundered what his new bride thought about his kitchen coffee making habit and how they made coffee in the pot after that.

Frank's housekeeping was something else. As I came up to his house, I would hear rifle fire. I wondered if it were safe to go in. As I ventured forth I would find Frank sitting in his favorite easy chair with his rifle in hand. A target would be in the corner of the living room. Ashes would be falling out of the stove and onto the floor. A lit hand-rolled cigarette would be adding interesting configurations of smoke to the room's atmosphere. It would be nice and cozy in the room, and Frank never seemed to be in any hurry to take the ashes outside. He would just sit back in his chair and shoot at the target whenever he felt like it.

I used to think, "My, Frank really knows how to live. He really has fun in life." To a young teenager, it probably did appear to be a wonderful fun-filled lifestyle.

When I was about ten years old, the barn on Frank's farm burned to the ground. Frank had made hay a few days earlier and had stored the hay in the barn. Hay must be very dry and fully cured or it will combust after it is stored. Frank had either put the hay in a little wet or a little too green, because it did ignite and the barn caught fire. I watched in awe and anxiety. I returned to the sanctum of my Shewman farm bedroom, but found myself thinking a lot about what I had just witnessed. I rolled and tossed in the old dark and lonesome upstairs of our house while attempting to find sleep.

Snake in the Bucket

From time to time, I would be employed by Frank to do his milking. I had this assignment during the time of Frank's intensive courting of his bride to be. She lived in Fort Wayne, some fifty miles distant. Frank would leave in early afternoon to make this trip. When evening came and his cows needed to be milked, I was there to do it.

There was one thing about milking cows; you had to do it on a regular schedule. Cows expected to be milked each morning and each night at about the same time. If you didn't it would affect the amount of milk they would give.

Frank kept a bucket to use in distributing ground feed to the cows. The bucket hung on a nail next to the ceiling of the cow barn. Frank had warned me to look carefully before taking the bucket down. Quite often, a black snake would coil itself in the bucket for a nap. The black snake was known for it's ability to devour rats, so Frank in no way wanted any harm to come to this snake. It was his friend. You can imagine how my heart must have pounded as I approached the bucket for the first time. Sure enough, I found Mr. Black Snake all curled up and having a nice snooze. I did not bother it and managed to find another bucket to use to dip feed when doing the chores for him.

Frank was one of the modern farmers and had milking machines. I liked to use this, except for having to put kickers on the stubborn cows. This was not much fun. Some cows caught on very quickly that we meant business. Others remained stubborn and eventually the farmer would sell them for beef.

All of the time that we lived at the Shewman farm, we did our milking by hand. About half of the farmers at that time had milking machines. During the time of World War ll, farmers started picking up from the Depression, and we saw evidence of some better times in new equipment being purchased. Newer and bigger tractors came on the scene.

Frank's School House Potatoes

Frank's farm was in close proximity to the Summit Lake chain. There were three lakes in the chain and Franks property bordered on two of them. There always seemed to be plenty of mystery as I worked in and about the fields of his farm. There were many trees and lots of underbrush that helped make the mystique of this area more appealing and fascinating to a young boy. The ground would shake as I would drive the tractor into some of the areas. Water is very close to the surface in most muck ground, making it very easy to get the tractor stuck. I had to be very careful. Frank had instructed me early in my working career to not let the wheels spin. If I did, he said "You may end up in China."

Muck ground is excellent for use in raising potatoes. Frank had a lot of muck ground. It was possible to drain some of the wet ground around the lakes with tile ditching, or sometimes by digging an open ditch. In any event, the ground would have to be drained toward an area that would receive the water. The drained ground would then become dry enough to plant. Frank had gained considerable tillable land through the draining process. I helped Frank plant potatoes in some of this newly acquired cultivatable land. After cultivating the potatoes several times during the summer growing period, we would harvest them in early fall. We called this part of the process "digging potatoes."

There was a lot more to it than simply digging potatoes. The potatoes had to be retrieved and stored in some fashion until they could be sold. Harvest time prices were not always the best. Frank knew when to sell to get the best price. He also knew that the potatoes had to be in good shape when he sold them.

Frank devised a piece of equipment that trailed behind the potato digger and caught the potatoes as they came out of the ground. I do not remember exactly how he came about this tool. The potatoes came up from the ground to a shaker-type conveyor chain belt. The shaker belt shook the dirt out and the potatoes proceeded to a bag that was in open position, hooked on the end of the shaker belt. One person stood on each side of the belt on a board similar to a running board. They threw out the potato vines as they passed in front of them. One person worked the rear where the potatoes were bagged. I found that I enjoyed this part of it the most. I would make sure the bags were full, tie them quickly with twine and set them off the bagger onto the ground. All of this would happen without the digger and bagger stopping.

Towards evening, with the help of Wayne Drudge, a local for hire trucker, we loaded the potatoes in bags and hauled them to the storage building, a vacant one room brick school house Frank had purchased. The building was on a small piece of land, located about two miles from his farm.

Another process that Frank pioneered in the potato business was brushing before storing. This function helped the potatoes to last better in storage and look better to a buyer when they were sold. As the potatoes were hauled to storage in bags, they were placed carefully into the brusher. They then found their way by chute to the basement storage area of the school building. This put the potatoes below grade and their chances of spoiling from the cold weather were much lessened. We were permitted to take time off from school to help in the harvesting of crops. I found much enjoyment in doing so. It was also a good source to add to my ever increasing need for spending money.

Frank and the C.C.C. Boys

During the early Thirties different work programs were started by the federal government to provide a means for some of the more unfortunate to feed their families. One such group was named the Civilian Conservation Corps. The popular short name for this group was the "C.C.C. boys." Our neighbor, Frank, seemed to be on the cutting edge of what was happening in the country, and particularly what might be of assistance to him on the farm. If a farmer could demonstrate his need and had the material available to do the job, he could make application to this program to receive labor from the C.C.C. boys.

Frank needed some fences to be constructed. He also asked to have some seedling trees planted. I can remember seeing large numbers of men loaded on trucks driving down Frank's long lane. They would spend the day splitting fence posts and then putting the posts into a large barrel standing on its side. The men had made a fire pit under the barrel. They put creosote in the barrel and let it boil for a while. The fence posts were placed in the boiling creosote for a specified amount of time. This treatment made the post last for years when placed in the ground.

All of this work by the C.C.C. boys happened before I started to work for Frank. After I started to work, I noticed much evidence of their labor. There were nice barbed wire fences all over the place and many young trees growing all around the farm.

When Frank's barn burned, he cut some of the larger trees on his farm. I got in on some of this tree cutting. Frank and I would saw the tree down with a crosscut saw. I was strong and young and had what I thought was lots of energy, but Frank was in his prime and could work the socks off me. I would have to make known my need for resting a lot sooner than he did. We loaded the logs onto a wagon by skids and hauled them up to the barnyard.

Eventually, there were enough logs accumulated. Frank called in a man named Paul Smiley who had a portable saw mill. My Dad helped Frank construct his new cow barn and hay storage from some of the Smiley sawn boards.

11

HIGH SCHOOL
and WORLD WAR ll

Rationing

Not long after World War ll started, we had the start of rationing. The fact that I lived in the country meant that gas rationing hit us the hardest. We did not use a tractor to farm with and this meant that we were not eligible for the farmer's "R" stamps. We did pump water for livestock with a gasoline engine and therefore qualified for a few "C" stamps. We kept the "C" stamp gas in a fifty gallon barrel. Dad was very particular about how this gas was used and would not allow any to be put into the automobile. He was very precise in what was right and what was wrong.

The automobile we were driving during this time period was a 33 Ford V-8. The "A" and the "B" gas stamps were displayed in the lower right corner of the windshield. The law was that you displayed the stamps. This allowed authorities the means to check your license plate to determine if you were too far from your residence for the kind of rationing stamp that you had displayed.

There were times that I wanted to go to town and there would not be enough gas in the car to get there and back. The gas gauge was not working but we had devised a method of measuring the tank with a stick. My mom would put a gallon or so of gas from the gas barrel into a little aluminum kettle and then pour the gas into the ol' "33". She knew full well what the consequences would be if my dad saw her do it. But she wanted me to have a few of the fun activities that she heard went on in town or at the school. She would just make sure that Dad was not in the barnyard or around the house where he might see. Mother's values were good, but she also was closer than Dad to the "real" things in life.

There were a few gas stations that had the reputation that they would accept most any kind of a stamp for gas. The fact that Akron was a farming community meant that the station could dispose of any kind of stamp. Some would take an "R" stamp that was supposed to be spent at the farm when the tractor barrel needed filling. A small community had its way of getting along and no one seemed to tattle on one another.

Shoes were rationed and also sugar. Mother would get a special allotment of sugar stamps to do her canning. This was expected of those living on the farm. I remember sugar coming to the house in large bags. Upstairs, the sugar would be placed on a large washing tub to keep the mice from bothering it. The flour was stored in the same room, using the same manner to protect it from the mice. We had lots of mice in those days.

Automobile tire rationing was the most visible and consequential of the rationing. With the war on and all of Uncle Sam's resources going into the war effort, getting new tire approval was just about impossible. To get by, we had to keep recapping over and over just as long as there was a side wall left on the tire that would take to the recapping process. Farmers could get permits to recap in order to carry on the business of farming. Farming was considered very essential to the war effort. Everything pivoted around the war effort.

Homer and the Scrap Drive

When World War ll started, it became very popular to show your patriotism. One way to do that was to participate in what we called "scrap drives." The defense factories were in full swing turning out planes, tanks, jeeps and all of the equipment of war. Uncle Sam wanted all of the scrap metal and aluminum we could lay our hands on. There was a neighbor by the name of Homer Saner who always kept a truck on his farm. Homer's truck was what we called an "open bed stake" of about one and a half ton classification.

One Saturday, Homer and his three boys came by our house. This was to be the first leg of their intended scrap drive. Homer wanted to know if I would go with them. Mom said I could. We searched the trash piles where we burned garbage, and gathered all of the scrap we could find, adding to that whatever pieces of iron or steel Dad could see fit to release. Then we set out to go over the neighborhood repeating the process of this patriotic search as we went from farm to farm. I can still hear Homer yelling, in his very strong voice as we approached each farm house, "Any bottles, any rags, any cans for Uncle Sam." I thought this to be pretty neat and really had a lot of fun doing it.

Homer drove a school bus and picked up school children in the Rock Lake area and on both sides of State Road #114 north of our farm and on into Akron. It was his custom to drive his school bus into Akron to all of the Akron High School home basketball games. I would walk the short distance to where he turned the corner just north of our farm and he would stop for me. I would pay him fifty cents a season for this privilege. It was a great way of entering in on all of the enthusiasm and support that went with living in a small Indiana community during basketball season. After I got into high school I found other ways to get there.

School Teachers Are Not All Bad

I have many happy thoughts of some of the school teachers that influenced my life. Some of them obviously made bigger impressions than others, but each was special. It is difficult to rank them, but each played a certain part in my growing up and in the education that was instilled in my young mind.

Miss Nellie Huppert was my first exposure to someone attempting to give me instruction outside of the home. Although the experiences with her are the furthest back in time, they still carry a bright image in my memory. She was also my second grade teacher. I'm sure having her two years in a row contributed to my long lasting memory of her.

Doris Arter, my third grade teacher, probably created the desire in me to have fun with mathematics. Eva Rowe taught me many basics in the fourth grade that have survived all these years.

Russell Shipley and Mr. Fox during the fifth and sixth grades, in spite of the apparent tempers that possessed them, were smart teachers that had zeroed in on the way to impart knowledge. I was so excited with fun made out of arithmetic assignments in the fifth grade that I finished the entire year's written homework in about three weeks. I repeated this action in the sixth grade. Both years found me after the first period, sitting in the office grading papers. I would be marking away with the red pencil given me, and both Mr. Shipley and Mr. Fox would forget that I was in the office. I would stay there until noon. I do not recall any other student loving to work with numbers with such vigor and having the privilege of being a teacher's aide. It didn't bother me that I was not doing class work along with my classmates on subjects that I would miss during the morning fun hours in the office.

I was privileged to learn under several teachers at the high school. They each ranked at different levels in my measurement. I recall Raymond Pontius and the way he made literature come alive. He would get excited about the tales of Edgar Allan Poe and would spend the entire class period keeping us on the edge of our seats. My first exposure to Shakespeare was in his classroom. I remember the entire class reading the parts to <u>A Midsummer Night's Dream</u>.

Mr. Pontius was wonderful with literature, but I had to wonder about his methods of keeping law and order. He would allow some of the boys to have snowball fights right in the room. Snow was outside the window on the window ledge. Some of the more rowdy boys raised the windows and helped themselves. Mr. Pontius would stack his books in a sort of fort around the front of his desk. It did not end there. He would busy himself by recording negative marks in his grade book against those involved in the snowball fight. There were other days of similar skirmishes. More and more negative marks were made in the book of record. When the grading period arrived, some of the boys had a lot of explaining to do at home.

George Cullers was a superior mathematics instructor and also made history a lot of fun. I had much pleasure in exercising my skills at the blackboard in competitive mathematics exercises. During the sessions of geometry, I became very interested in proving triangles congruent. Three theorems were accepted at that time, but I developed a fourth. I became known to the class as a "geometry theorist." Mr.Cullers became a very good friend. I played many games of ping-pong with him, and he taught me many good moves.

World War ll was in full swing. Several teachers went off to war. We lost our principal, Mr. Meredith, to Uncle Sam. Dwight Gallip took over and I had many chances to work with him in various administrative assignments during the last two years of high school. I was the class president both junior and senior years.

I convinced my Latin teacher, Miss Morrison, that I was used to getting only an A+ and she went for it. That is what I received the first grading period. I must confess, that was the only A+ that made it to my report card.

Al Mathiesen will be remembered for all of the fun times he made happen in and out of the agriculture classes. These included the many pest contests that found us farm boys collecting sparrow and crow heads, rat and mice tails. We divided into two teams and started carrying in those parts of pests that counted so many points each. The agriculture room started to take on a sorry odor after the first week of accumulating some of the interesting contest trophies.

Mr. Mathiesen, in his absence, of course, was fondly referred to as "Ol' Hammerhead." What a nice guy. He worked very hard and I think he earned every dollar they paid to him.

When the corn had matured in the local fields, we would have corn husking contests. This came under the umbrella of the agriculture class and was staged at one of the farms in the area. We had the choice of being a contestant and shucking corn or be a gleaner and going behind the shuckers to look for what they might miss. We usually did this on a beautiful sunny fall day. It was fun.

The local 4-H Club put on exciting judging contests, and I participated in the poultry and egg contests. I got to travel about the state to different poultry farms. I got pretty good at candling eggs and determining just how old the eggs were. I could look at a laying hen's posterior and tell you just how busy the hen had been in the egg nest in the henhouse.

High School Days and World War ll

The high school building was located on the north edge of Akron. The building had four levels, and accommodated grades seven through twelve. The south side of the building had the lockers and most of the class rooms for grades seven and eight. I thought that I was big stuff when I left the grade school building and started attending the high school. For one thing, we had a different room for each subject. We got to get up and move about. The seventh and eighth grades were called junior high.

I was introduced to organized basketball and played on the junior high team. It was a big transition from shooting an old oil can or a stuffed softball to a real air filled basketball. They used real leather balls with an opening for the bladder to go into, laced with a leather thong.

I was really amazed at all of the equipment that the coach had at his disposal. I couldn't believe the fancy air pump the coach used to inflate the balls. I hardly knew what white surgical tape was. Here I saw many rolls of it all in one place. I discovered that the coach used the tape for many things, not just for cut fingers. We never purchased any of this kind of tape on the farm. If we injured a finger, we simply wrapped a piece of clean rag around the cut and doused it with turpentine or coal-oil. It burned like fire, but I grew up thinking that was what you had to do to keep on living. Mom would warn me that if I didn't treat the cut this way, I might get lockjaw or, worse yet, lose my finger.

One day of each school year was given to track and field events. I grew up throwing clods of dirt and rocks around on the farm. I got pretty accurate in heaving them quite a distance, making them land in a certain spot. Naturally, I moved into the shot-put event when it came around. I did very well in this sport. Seems to me I was as good as anyone else.

I did not care too much for calisthenics. I put up with them, knowing that softball and basketball were around the corner. Softball was my best sport. I played third base during my junior year. Earl Rodgers was playing shortstop when he was a senior. When Earl graduated, I moved to shortstop.

Some of the games were played on the other school's diamond and about half of the games were played behind Leininger's General Store on the town ball diamond. It was a nice lighted field, one of the better ones around.

We played most of the high school games immediately after school and did not have much need for the lights. When our team was the traveling team we would usually cut classes short, leaving in time to be at the other school diamond at the end of their school day.

Prior to the war days, high school sports teams were transported in school buses. Each school bus driver owned his truck chassis and bus body. The high school principal would contract with one of the drivers to transport the team players to the away games. After World War ll started, gas rationing followed and the use of buses halted. The coach and the more interested teachers would find gas stamps somewhere and drive their cars to haul the players. I did not get to travel much in those days, so going to the games was great fun. We played within a thirty mile radius.

Some of the longer trips required me to stay after school in order to be ready for the departure of the caravan of cars. I would get out of chore duties at home for that evening and this meant no milking the cows. I am not so sure Dad approved of all of this activity. Mom had a way of mediating that reassured Dad that what I was doing was essential and that they should allow me to be involved.

I recall the players on my senior year softball team. We ended the season undefeated. Garland Eshelman played center field and could throw a runner out at home plate without the catcher, Bill Hill, moving an inch.

Some of the double plays would involve Gordon Groninger at third, Snork Nye at second, and Gene Burch at first. Of course, I was in the middle of things at shortstop.

Morey Utter, George Harper, and Wayne Groninger were the rest of the outfield. Dick Landis was our pitcher and disappointed many a batter, thinking he was going to get a hit. If they hit the ball, it usually would go to the infield. This made more activity for me at shortstop. I loved to make the double plays and throw them out at first. Catching a line drive was a thrill, also. These were fun times for me. Through the many years since, I have allowed some very fine details to live on in some of my fondest memories.

It was common practice for those that could afford it to purchase a class ring the junior year. The ring the boys selected was larger than the girl's ring. The set was made of black onyx with AHS in the middle. I was able to save up enough to make the purchase. The cost was ten dollars and eighty-seven cents.

Downtown With Current Affairs
and "Square Root"

As I grew older I was allowed to stay after school for various functions. In the fall, this might mean a softball game or practice time. Later in the year, basketball became king and took center stage. There would be class play practice for some during the junior and senior years.

A couple of doors east of the downtown square of Akron, on Main Street, was the "Eat Rite Cafe." This establishment was the favorite hang-out for many of us. If we had an activity immediately after school, we would gather at the cafe afterward.

On the west wall of the cafe stood the popular juke box. All of the big band sounds of Glenn Miller, Harry James, Tommy and Jimmy Dorsey could be purchased for a nickel or six for a quarter. I did not have many nickels available for these sounds, but I sure enjoyed the records of those who could afford them.

Sometimes I would purchase a hamburger for ten cents and a glass of milk for a nickel. For fifteen cents I could manage very nicely. If I felt a little rich, I would spend another dime and buy a piece of chocolate pie.

In front of the cafe, just below the large plate glass window, was a cement ledge. The ledge provided an excellent bench to sit on and discuss current affairs. Subject matter for current affairs might include the latest gossip about certain girls and what they would or would not do. It might be that one of our older classmates was thinking about enlisting into military service. We would debate the pros and cons of that situation. We only used the bench in good weather. The cold weather of Indiana would quickly chase us inside to the warmth of the cafe.

One particular classmate, who had started the first grade with me, had an unusual ability of recalling at an instant the square root of any number randomly given to him. This ability was not recognized in him during the earlier grades but became evident in his early teens. When this young man was not spouting off square roots he might be persuaded to count the number of railroad ties between Akron and Disco, or maybe even Laketon. Some of the fellows would do such devilish things as to have "Square Root",as I called him, stand flat-footed under the cafe sign and try to jump up and touch it.

Sometimes Square Root would be convinced that if he were to make a running approach from the east end of Akron he would have a better chance of touching the sign. One time he was persuaded to start his approach from the north edge of Akron coming down State Highway Nineteen. To do this he had to break his stride and turn a corner just before approaching the sign. This did not deter Square Root in the slightest. He always seemed to believe he could do something if the fellows around him thought he could. His report card gave him positive consideration only in the area of arithmetic and mathematics. It was no surprise to any of us when Square Root quit school.

I always wondered what happened to him after he quit school. Recently, I learned that he had married and had a lovely talented family and lived somewhere in the community.

EPILOGUE

As I look backwards into some of the furthest recesses of my mind, I see the stark, knife scarred desks of the old assembly hall of Akron High. Who could predict what the current events that were announced that mid-day in December, 1941, would play in some of our futures?

As I sat in one of the desks, pondering some class assignment, President Roosevelt brought us the news over the assembly speaker system that we were at war with Japan. I did not fully realize what was around the corner for me.

A son of a farmer in those days quite often continued in his father's footsteps and became a farmer. Very few went to college. No one had any money to pay tuition.

257

Some drifted off to the big city and found work in factories. But even that was not easy before World War ll.

As I continued on through high school, I kept thinking about my future, wondering just what foxhole or shipmine would do me in. I did not consider college or the opportunities that a completed education might offer. The war effort was not limited to just making bombs and tanks and killing people. Patriotism captured our entire person and most young men thought only of serving their country. Young farm lads were no exception. The youth within us always managed to find small disks of pleasure that came our way. We did have some laughs, some pleasures of growing up and learning what it was to think adult.

The special day of high school graduation came in April, 1944. As I sat through all of the speeches and accumulated my share of perspiration, I was starting to make decisions about what I would do with my immediate future. Thirty-four of us accepted the diploma of completion from our high school. All of us knew that this was a big milestone in our lives. We each left the building that evening, for the most part not to see one another again for decades.

The few short weeks of summer between graduation and when I left for Naval service in August, all sped by so fast. My opportunities to observe my mother and to hear her advice were coming to an end. None of us had the knowledge Mother would leave us so soon. She died the following summer while I was in the North Pacific.

When I recall those early mornings watching my mother scurry around in the kitchen on the Shewman farm, I noted how she demonstrated her sensitivity to life. The church hymns of her youth continued into her adulthood as welcome beacons of hope. She would hum the familiar assurances of the hymns as she moved about our kitchen preparing breakfast for my dad, my brothers, my sister and, of course, me.

Perhaps the early lessons of money management that I observed while sitting at Mother's knee in front of the north window of this same kitchen were the foundation of what I have taught my children. Mom always made things seem so right and that it was proper for me to want something. She usually found a way for me to receive my small boy desires.

Maybe it was watching my dad improvise when he had no money to go to Akron and purchase a replacement for a broken tool from Secor's or Miller's hardwares.

Or maybe it is the memories that I have of his long days in the fields and short nights on the old straw tick and then the next day repeat it all again. I know now he did it for me. All through my life I have been careful to not waste, to follow Dad's example and "make some things do."

Mom told me to never forget the happenings about me. The small and the large events that crossed my path could serve a worthwhile purpose in making good judgments later in life. To this day I practice some of the unrecorded advice of hers that only memories can flush to the sides of the roads of life I now travel. I find much comfort in my life in practicing the same spiritual faiths she demonstrated to me.

As I chronicled this trail of time of a young boy's life from a meager farm beginning, I became aware of the many opportunities that came my way. The consistent advice to those simple questions of life Dad and Mom gave to me while living on the Shewman farm remain as my road map today. I will always remember with fondness the many hours of family sharing, as we watched the Indiana daylight become night while we were sitting on the washroom linoleum covered floor.

To this day, I cannot pass a produce department in the local supermarket without stopping by the watermelons. Those memories of hawking Dad's home-grown melons in the front yard of the Shewman farm still live on. Cookies that I see in the bakery section of that same store sometimes remind me of the mud pies I bartered to my nephews for lilac leaves.

I like to think even my early play business venture helped prepare me for the life that was ahead. In all of my lifetime work assignments, along with corporate administrative responsibilities, I have had the opportunity of handling millions of dollars through banks all around the world using satellite communications systems. I am convinced that this type of communication is a million light years away from the dry-cell battery powered wall phone, hanging on the north wall of the kitchen on the old Shewman farm.

Yes, my mom was a genius. "Remember it all, Billy," she would say. I tried to do just that.

261

To Order Additional Copies Of:

FROM MUD PIES and LILAC LEAVES

Send $19.95 U.S. Currency
Plus $3.00 Shipping & Handling
For each Copy
(Add tax where appropriate)

Make Funds Payable to:
Honeybil Publishing
P.O. Box 2806
Clackamas, OR 97015